C000004607

CORBYN'

Edited by
Tom Unterrainer

Jeremy Corbyn MP
Umaar Kazmi
Abi Rhodes
Ben Sellers
Christine Shawcroft
Tony Simpson
Nadia Whittome
Adele Williams
Chris Williamson

SPOKESMAN
Nottingham

First published in 2016

Spokesman
Russell House, Bulwell Lane,
Nottingham, NG6 0BT, England
www.spokesmanbooks.com

ISBN 978 085124 851 6

A cataloguing-in-publication (CIP) record is available
from the British Library

Printed and bound in Nottingham by Russell Press Ltd
www.russellpress.com   0115 9784505

Contents

Introduction *Tom Unterrainer*   5

PART 1 – VOICES OF THE CAMPAIGN

1. Building a Social Movement *Jeremy Corbyn MP*   9
2. Closing the Moral Defecit *Umaar Kazmi*   20
3. The People's Party *Nadia Whittome*   22

PART 2 – CAMPAIGN AND VICTORY

4. #JezWeDid *Ben Sellers*   27
5. After the 2015 General Election *Chris Williamson*   40
6. Labour's Rules *Christine Shawcroft*   57
7. Remaking the Labour Party *Adele Williams*   64
8. The 'Unelectable' Elected Man *Abi Rhodes*   71

PART 3 – CHANGING OUR WORLD?

9.   The Motive Force of Empire *Jeremy Corbyn MP*   79
10. Internationalist at Work *Tony Simpson*   88
11. Socialist Renewal and Workers' Control *Tom Unterrainer* 103

APPENDICES – CAMPAIGN POLICIES

The Economy in 2020; Housing;   116
Defence Diversification; Protecting our Planet

Introduction

Tom Unterrainer

Defying all expectations, Jeremy Corbyn was elected Labour Leader with a resounding mandate. His campaign re-wrote the rules of British politics by mobilising tens of thousands of supporters both within and outside the Party. The 'Corbyn for Leader' campaign, a radical social movement reflecting aspects of the new left that has emerged across Europe, and Jeremy's ultimate victory provide the rarest of opportunities to redefine socialism and the Labour Party for a new generation.

This book aims to serve two purposes. First, as a record of how – against all odds – a long-serving socialist Member of Parliament came to be Leader of the Labour Party. Second, to provoke and organise debate by asking challenging questions about the road ahead of us. There are no detailed proposals or political demands within these pages – as urgent as such formulations are, we aim for something more open-ended in this volume. We do, however, re-print the policy statements issued by Jeremy's campaign throughout the contest to indicate possible departure points for further debate and discussion.

Each contribution expresses a personal view: there is no uniformity of opinion other than a commitment to celebrating Jeremy Corbyn's success and seizing the opportunities that now exist. This collection opens with three contributions made at 'Corbyn for Leader' rallies in Nottingham. The first is from Jeremy himself, who spoke to a packed room of Labour Party members, anti-austerity and anti-war activists at the very start of his campaign. The other two contributions are from young Labour Party members. Their voices and opinions had a powerful effect on the second Nottingham rally, later in the campaign, and we are honoured to re-print their speeches.

Chris Williamson, Labour MP for Derby until the 2015 election, should be playing a central role in the Parliamentary Labour Party and a leading role in the Party at large. Deprived of this opportunity by 41 votes, Chris is nevertheless an important voice in the struggle to renew the Party. His contribution focuses on the reasons for Labour's defeat in 2015 and Jeremy's victory in the subsequent leadership contest. Christine Shawcroft is a longstanding member of Labour's National Executive Committee. Her contribution sheds light on the importance of Labour's Rulebook and indicates what changes are required to open up the internal democracy of the party.

Ben Sellers and Adele Williams paint vivid picture of Jeremy's campaign itself, albeit from very different perspectives. Whilst Ben focuses on the vital role played by social media throughout the campaign, Adele describes the transformational opportunities presented to local Labour Party organisation as a result of the campaign.

Abi Rhodes examines how Jeremy Corbyn and the Party he now leads have been characterised in the media. Tony Simpson reflects on the importance of Jeremy's internationalist outlook, with particular attention to Trident and to Syria.

Whilst aiming for a Labour victory in 2020 (or sooner, it must be hoped) by re-building and re-organising the Party, we should also aim to engage in an open process of debate, discussion and socialist renewal. At times, the world appears a dark and forbidding place. Jeremy's victory has potentially ignited a process where some light can be shed on the world. Such a process will be the work of many thousands of people, many of whom may have no idea of the vitally creative roles they will play in times to come.

PART 1

Voices from the Campaign

1
Building a Social Movement
Jeremy Corbyn MP

On Sunday 28 June 2015, Jeremy Corbyn spoke at the first of what eventually became one hundred campaign rallies. This first rally was organised by the Bertrand Russell Peace Foundation, together with anti-war and anti-austerity campaigners in Nottingham. Jeremy later told the BBC's Robert Peston, 'we knew something was happening when a hundred people turned up on a Sunday lunchtime in Nottingham at 24 hours' notice'. NG Digital broadcast the event and a recording is available on their website, from which Nicole Morris transcribed the following text.

Thanks very much for inviting me along today, and thank you all for coming, because one thirty on a Sunday afternoon doesn't sound the ideal time for a public meeting to me! But thanks for being here, and it's great to come in and see Ken Coates' books there on the table, and it's great to see the former Nottingham South MP, my great friend Alan Simpson, and I'm really sorry he's not in Parliament with me now. He would have probably cautioned lots of things on this but would have been very supportive of what we're doing – thank you, Alan.

I just want to set out the basis on which we're running this campaign. Like everyone here I was devastated by the general election result. We lost; there were many inadequacies in the Labour campaign – I'll come back to those in a moment; but fundamentally the Tories used money, greed, individualism and nastiness in order to create a sufficiently large number of votes to give themselves a parliamentary majority. Their parliamentary majority is based on a low turnout, it's based on the support of 24% of the electorate as a whole, and if you look at what they're now planning to do, it is quite appalling in any way whatsoever. The cancellation of the East Midlands train line upgrade – the development to the Midland Main Line – is just one example of the stuff they said they would do before the election which they're now going to change completely.

When they announced the first budget after the 2010 election, the first thing they did was to take a scythe to the benefits budget, and this time they're doing exactly the same: they're going take another twelve billion off that budget. But they're setting this up in quite a clever way, because they're now provoking a parliamentary vote on whether or not there should be a reduction in the benefit cap from £25,000 maximum to £23,000 maximum. I'll make no bones about it: I'm going to vote against any benefit cap, because it is the wrong way to treat people. But the amount of money involved in the benefit cap is actually very small compared to all the other cuts that are due to take place in the benefit budget, and areas like mine are greatly affected by it.

I represent an inner city, high-cost area where private sector rents are routinely £300-400 a week for a two bedroom flat, £1000 a week for a house. It's astronomical, way beyond the benefit level, therefore there is a social cleansing of the whole of central London. People say 'that's London, that's the South, that's different' – yes, but the principle is the same everywhere, and it if can happen in London it can happen anywhere in the future. It's a whole principle about how we approach these things. And so my answer to wasting money on housing benefit is cut the rent bill by controlling private sector rents, particularly starting in London and the South East. We're mounting a big campaign on that, to try and get a London opt-out in the next piece of housing legislation, to give an elected London Mayor the power to control and regulate private tenancies, and if we achieve that – which we might do – that'll be a huge step forward, so there's plenty of issues there.

But the other points in the election campaign were surely this: that the Liberal Democrats were clearly on the way down; Labour made some good points – Ed Miliband made some very good points about zero-hours contracts, about right to work, about young people's opportunities, about poverty wages and so on – very good stuff indeed, but the problem was that the fundamental economic strategy of the Party was a form of austerity-lite.

Before the election I went to my local authority, Islington Council, and I said 'give me the scenarios of what happens after the general election'. They said 'how many scenarios do you want?' I said three: 'Coalition government re-elected; Labour government elected; Tory government elected'.

They said:
'Coalition government elected: big cuts.
Tory government elected: huge cuts.
Labour government elected: smaller cuts.'

But there were still cuts, of millions and millions of pounds. Nottingham has lost – what, a hundred million? And you can multiply that all over the country, and the scythe that's now being taken to local government spending all over the country is going to create a massive adult social care crisis. Adult social care is expensive, for good reason, and important for obvious reasons, and it takes up more and more of local government expenditure, and will take up more and more – every other service is going to be cut, until such time as adult social care itself is also cut. The solution of privatising, opting out, contracting out services, may buy a little bit of time, may buy short-termism, but in the long run it's not going to solve the issue. The issue has to be the amount of public money that is spent on public services.

Now, why do we accept this argument of austerity? The 2008-9 banking crisis – what brought that about? Was it the profligacy of the school cleaners, and the nurses, and everybody else? And those people that fix the roads and stuff like that getting excessively high wages? Or was it an unregulated banking system brought about on top of a sub-prime mortgage crisis in the United States that brought about a banking collapse? The response of the government – and I remember sitting there in parliament watching – I couldn't believe the figures being read out! When Alistair Darling came and made a statement saying we're going to put 25 something-or-other into a bank, I said to the MP sitting next to me, 'how much did he say?' He said '25'; I said '25 what – million or billion?'; he said '... I think it's billion'; I said 'Are you sure? Get the written version of the statement!' (because the written version of the statement comes around shortly after the oral version's been made). Yes, it was £25 billion – unbelievable.

Suddenly, £25 billion comes from nowhere to go into banks, and that was only the start. And then day after day, statements came with more and more money going in to prop up the banking system, and then came the magic moment of nationalising the banks. Now, when I joined the Young Socialists in the 1960s, we used to have wet dreams about nationalising the banks! Do you remember: '[nationalise] the two hundred banks and insurance companies'? I used to think 'wow!' And then the vote came to nationalise the banks! And I thought 'I'm going to be there! I want to be recorded! I'm going to be voting to nationalise the banks'. *There was not even a vote!* There was nobody voting against it. And then of course you go into the details of why, and what we did was we took out a very large public share in the banks, but we didn't take control of the banks, and the shares are held by a wholly government-owned holding company whose duty it is to sell the shares when they reach a particular price. And Osborne is now selling RBS shares at a £1.50 per share loss, compared to what they were bought for at that time. This was all about propping up a banking system rather than taking control of a banking system, and the austerity continues.

What's been the product of austerity over the past five years? Greater and greater poverty, greater and greater inequality in our society; running parallel to that, a media strategy of blaming the poor for their poverty, and blaming the poor for the excessive level of the benefit bill. *Benefits Street* and bank bail-outs are part of the same equation and part of the same issue that we're judging at the present time. Inequality, I can give you lots of figures but I'll give you one, just hold this in your mind for a moment: the richest 100 people in Britain own the equivalent of a third of the wealth of the entire population, and it's getting worse. We have tax havens around Europe, we have tax havens around the world, and, according to Richard Murphy, we have £100 billion a year not collected in tax that should be collected from big corporations. These are the issues we have to face. Now, I think in the election, the problem was that at the end of it, could we honestly say to public sector workers: 'Your wages are going to go up, the pay freeze is going to be limited, we're going to end the privatisation and contract culture in public services', or not? No. We couldn't in all honesty say that. And so nobody, no working class people particularly wanted a Tory government, but out of desperation they did a number of things. Young people, 53% of whom did not vote in the election (of those that registered), stayed home. Older people voted in somewhat larger numbers, but we lost support in a number of ways. We lost support to UKIP, in England, particularly.

I was spending quite a lot of time campaigning in Thanet South because I like the air around Margate, I like the seaside, and I particularly dislike Nigel Farage. So what was there not to enjoy about going to Thanet during the election? And some of the conversations I had were utterly bizarre, where the UKIP narrative that every problem was the fault of immigration, the European Union, and all you could see for posters was pictures of the white cliffs of Dover and you could hear Vera Lynn singing, and that was going to sort it all out. I was saying to people 'hang on a minute. UKIP: are they actually going to build any houses? Are they actually going to provide any new hospitals? Are they actually going to provide more school places? Are they going to do anything other than give you a feel-good factor, so that you can blame somebody else who is as poor or poorer than you, for the situation you're all in?' We need to build a bit of unity between people, and remember the watchword of what the Labour Movement and Trade Unions are about. It's about unity. We need to build that sense of unity between all workers, whatever their status, wherever they work, so we build a stronger Labour Movement. That is the best way of defeating UKIP and the racism that underlies some of their message.

But we also lost some votes to the Greens, partly maybe on environmental issues, but I think it was actually more to do with the Greens giving an anti-austerity message, and we did lose support for that even in constituencies where those people voting Green knew full well that it was clearly damaging the chances in a first-past-the-post system of Labour winning those constituencies. So is the solution to blame the Greens for existing, or is the solution to look at the policies that Labour was putting forward in this election?

When we examined all this straight after the election, we had a meeting in London at the NUT offices, they very kindly gave us the space to do it straight after the election, and we went through all the things that had happened. We then discussed what we would do about the post-election period, whether there was to be a leadership contest or not, because Ed Miliband had already resigned as leader. The general view was that we wouldn't get the 35 signatures necessary to get anyone on the ballot paper, therefore we'd shelve that one and we'd concentrate on policy. I then spoke at the Parliamentary Labour Party meeting the following week, as did other colleagues on the Left saying that there should not be a leadership contest, that Harriet Harman as deputy leader should carry on as acting leader, should carry on for six months, nine months, a year, whatever – so we could have that fundamental debate about the economic and international directions of the party. Sadly, the National Executive instead put in quite a long leadership election campaign but didn't really give space for that policy review. So we then discussed the issue again and I was asked if I was prepared to put my name above the parapet and see what happened. And so I did and found we had 11 people supporting my name going above the parapet. We then discovered I hadn't nominated myself, so I decided I would nominate myself and that put it up to 12, but we were still quite a long way off the number we needed. And then what happened was a very interesting thing.

The fact is it's not about me: it's about us, it's about a movement, it's about people, it's about ideas, it's about people looking for some collective way forward. We then got amazing numbers of people working on Facebook, Twitter and social media to start a campaign saying 'the voice of the Left should be on the ballot paper, we should be heard'. And we obviously asked various MPs to nominate us; some nominated on the basis that they thought it was a good idea, others were very reluctant to, but there was pressure from a lot of people all over the country and a lot of MPs … I say thank you to those MPs that did nominate me who profoundly disagree with me but felt the democratic process should take place and there should be that debate. And so the numbers agonisingly crept up a bit, but by Monday morning we were still on 18, and that was with four hours to go, so we weren't over-confident at that stage. And then I started doing various BBC interviews, and one of them said:

'Well it says here you're on 27', and I said 'No, that's wrong, it's 28'. He said 'how do you know?'

'I've just had a text.'

'Are you sure? Show it to me!'

So we were building the numbers up, and at the last moments of the thing, and then with two minutes to go we were on 33. And at that point somebody comes gleefully out of Sky News, because I was in Millbank – 'ah, you haven't done it, you haven't done it!' I said 'you just wait 'til the fat lady sings! Just see what happens'. And he said 'yeah, ok'. Then I went back over to the room, and we'd got it with 120 seconds to spare, the last nominations went in, so we got on the ballot paper. And that is an achievement for those people who supported us all over the country by pressurising their MP to make that nomination.

So, we're on the ballot paper. We now have all these hustings debates going on, and it's amazing the numbers of people attending them. We had 1,200 in Birmingham yesterday – hundreds of people, very large attendances to all of these. They're all on a set format, it's a slightly wooden format because there's an independent chair, usually a journalist, we draw lots of the order of answering, and the order of summing up at the end. 30 seconds to ask a question, 1 minute to answer, and so we go on and there's usually 9 or 10 questions at each of these hustings, which is not very many, and we then get two minutes to reply at the end of it. Actually, it's good that we're having them, it's good that members can put questions in, but I think it's unfortunate we're not having either a chance for the questioner to come back and say 'Well, I don't agree with any of the answers I was given', or 'I agree with all of them', or to make some other point – I just think it would be more interactive to do that. I also think it would be much better if we had themed discussions and themed debates, so that we had an hour, for example, on economic policy and so you could actually go into the whole principles behind austerity, and what's going on behind it, and what the alternative arguments are; go through it and have that debate. Likewise, on international affairs, but we are stuck with this. But what it has done is opened up an awful lot of space and an awful lot of debate. And I've never known so many people in my constituency stop me in the street and say 'Jeremy, the point about austerity and the economic thing – I've always thought this …'

I said, 'Yep. Great. Good. What are you going to do about it?'

He said: 'Well yeah, what you need to say is this …'

Well fine, that's good! People are at last talking about politics because they can see a debate going on in the Labour Party.

There is a fairly small political party membership in Britain, really. The Labour Party membership is, give or take some, around 240,000. I've no idea what the Conservative Party membership figure is; they don't admit it but they claim it's bigger than that, but I have my doubts. Liberal Democrat membership I have no idea; I suspect it's not very big. And so there isn't a vast number of people in political parties in Britain, but that's not to say we're living in a totally depoliticised society. Look at the 250,000 that came on the anti-austerity march last weekend; look at the vast number who were on the Pride march in London yesterday, and the demonstration. People *are* involved in politics in a different way: they're involved in justice campaigns, they're involved in causes, they're involved in peace movements, they're not necessarily involved in political parties.

I think we need to build a social movement. We need to build a social movement that brings together the economic issues that I've been talking about now, but also brings together the peace issues, and I'll finish with this point. The Stop the War movement, we founded that in 2001, not because of Iraq – Iraq hadn't even been thought of at that stage – but because of the invasion of Afghanistan. We had three and a half thousand people [come] to that launch meeting at Friends Meeting House. It was an incredible event and we then built that Stop the War movement, and we're still around, and I suspect we're going to be around for a very long time. I'm the chair of Stop the War Coalition at the moment, and very happy to be so, because we bring together a coalition of people who look at the world in a different way. And so when I was asked a question this morning at the hustings – 'what do you think about what's happened in Tunisia?', 'what do you think about ISIS?' and so on – my broad reply was this: obviously what happened in Tunisia was beyond appalling. There are many people in Tunisia, young people, who want to live in a secular democratic society, are fed up with poverty, with unemployment, with graduating into unemployment, and living quite difficult lives. Some of those see a solution in something very different which isn't about uniting people, it's about doing something else and that's what the awful event was yesterday. But I say this: had we not gone into Afghanistan, had we not invaded Iraq, had we not lined up with Bush and the neocons on the War on Terror, would ISIS now exist? Would ISIS now be so well funded? Would ISIS now be using weapons provided by the United States, particularly, but by other countries as well, that were probably sold via Qatar, Bahrain and Saudi Arabia, or not? I say to you that what we've done by the War on Terror is created Islamophobia, we've created a division in the world, and we've created massive migrant refugee flows of desperate people trying to escape war who are now being told they're not welcome in Europe, even though they've managed to survive getting across the Mediterranean on some kind of leaky boat.

What's our answer to this? To say that austerity is caused by the poor taking too much in benefits? That war is caused by Palestinian people trying to survive? Or are we going to say, instead, that the real issues facing this world are the refugee flows, the environmental disaster, the wars, the catastrophe, the arms trade, and the grab of natural resources from people in the poorest countries in the world? Are we instead to look to a global vision? We don't join in with UKIP in attacking migrants. We don't join in with the Right in blaming the poor for their poverty. Instead, we lift our eyes up.

The Labour Party was founded by people who had a fantastic vision of a different world. I was reading a lot about the works of Keir Hardie, and he sounds like he was a really awkward guy – he was probably very nice underneath it all – but he had this absolute steely determination that he was going to build a political party that would represent the working class. That's what his whole life was about. He died, sadly, a broken man after the xenophobia of the First World War had taken over and he'd been effectively politically sidelined because of his anti-war stance – later rehabilitated after his death, by the way. It often happens to people.

New Labour didn't follow any of those traditions. New Labour hollowed out the party. New Labour damaged the democratic structures of the party. New Labour took away our policy-making options within the party. And so in this debate I'm saying a few things. One: austerity – I've said that. Two: internationalism and opposition to nuclear weapons, and Trident renewal in absolutely any form whatsoever. Three: a constitutional convention for the whole of the UK so we work out what the relationship is between England-Wales-Scotland-Northern Ireland, English regions, work out a voting system, work out all those things, *bring people in* to that debate; but also, return to democratic policy making within the Labour Movement so unions will want to affiliate to the Labour Party, others will want to be part of the Labour Party, so we can build from bottom up a different economic strategy in which the sole objective is to reduce inequality and eliminate poverty within our society. In that we can achieve a great deal, and if this campaign achieves nothing else, I hope it mobilises a lot of people into a social movement where we can march down the road together against austerity and for peace, and if that is all we can achieve that'll be great. If we achieve more, that's even better.

Umaar Kazmi and Nadia Whittome spoke at the second 'Corbyn for Leader' rally in Nottingham, eight weeks later, on 20 August 2015. Guardian columnist Michael White reported on the rally the next day:

> 'Two teenage speakers, Nadia Whittome and Umaar Kazmi, attacking the "lies, deceit and warmongering" of the Blair/Brown era of their childhood, and the Cameron era's zero-hours contracts, were startlingly fluent.'

Umaar and Nadia didn't only make an impression on Michael White, but also on the thousand-strong crowd in attendance at the Albert Hall.

2
Closing the Moral Defecit
Umaar Kazmi

I was born on 16 April 1997, during the final two weeks of John Major's Government and, indeed, the dying days of Conservative control over our country. And, clearly, I was far too young to have experienced the euphoria, the hope, and the high expectations that the country had with a Labour Party that had been in opposition for 18 years and had just won 418 seats in a landslide election. The country was waiting, and expecting to be reshaped in a different and better mould.

But, whilst I was only an infant then, I *was* old enough to feel the deep-seated anger shared by many towards Tony Blair and then Gordon Brown during the dying days of *their* government. Because, back then, all I *believed* about Labour was that it was a party of lies, deception and warmongering. It was the reason why so many people were concerned and felt suspicious about my religion and why so many people were angry about 'immigrants' who were supposedly taking all their jobs.

I was 13 years old at that time and I actually felt relieved when David Cameron and Nick Clegg stood in front of 10 Downing Street on 11 May 2010. Relief that I clearly don't feel now, I can assure you. Now, at this point, I think it's important for me to say: vast swathes of Labour Party supporters were passionately against many of the actions taken by our last two Prime Ministers. I don't doubt that there are people in this room who were down in London on 15 February 2003 to make their voices heard against the invasion of Iraq. But, just like the majority of people in this country, you weren't listened to, and so people *like me* were particularly affected. I'm not going to argue that Muslims are a wholly united, single-minded block because we're not. But one area where we *were* unified was our support of the Labour Party. The ideals of equality, tolerance, and, most importantly, social justice are at the very core of what we are and what we believe. But these values were misrepresented and undermined through false pretexts used to justify needless wars, and the Labour Party lost the trust of millions of people, and the bitter resentment of those years still exists in the hearts of many people, and many people have still not forgiven Labour.

And then, an individual arises from the backbenches and dispels that resentment. An individual whose principles and integrity allowed *him* to resist and campaign against the wars in Iraq and Afghanistan, an individual whose ethics, humility and tolerance fills the heart of a pessimist with hope for the future. He's somebody who I believe is not only in the best position to regain the support of the most marginalised communities in this country, but the *only* person capable of inspiring everyone who was left behind under Blair, Brown, and now Cameron. Everyone who feels no party represents them. Everyone who believes all politicians are the same. Everyone who wants to see a Labour Party that *truly* believes in equality, tolerance and social justice.

This is Labour's time to reclaim its stake in those communities that have been damaged, violated and beaten down by successive governments that have failed them. The Tories spread their rhetoric about the deficit. Fine, they've got five more years to fail again. But it should be *our* job, in *this* Party, to finally close the *moral* deficit left by New Labour.

So, that's why it's not only a privilege, but actually my deepest honour to stand before you to ask everyone, but especially those who are still angry with the Labour Party, to give your support to the politician whose principals have remained unshaken through 32 years of being in Parliament. If that only says one thing about Jeremy Corbyn, it says that this man is committed to the ideals and values of a true and honest Labour Party that we can all support and believe in.

3
The People's Party
Nadia Whittome

I'm incredibly honoured to be sharing a platform with such eminent speakers and, of course, our future prime minister! I'm 18 years old and one of nearly seven million young people in the UK. As young people, either we're paying high tuition fees and accruing massive debt, or we are caught in the trap of low paid work, have a zero hours contract, or no job at all. Or all of the above.

None of us aspire to claim benefits. We all want to earn money, and to actively participate in the economy, but we need to be equipped with the tools: training, jobs, and a proper wage; not 'work boot camps' to 'earn' benefits.

I've cast my vote for Jeremy Corbyn because he has a vision for young people, not just the 50% of us attending university, but also the other three-and-a-half million, who may not be represented here this evening. I applaud Jeremy's strategy for lifelong learning. Without Access courses like mine, those with potential are denied the opportunity to pursue higher education. Or take the example of my brother, now 27 years old, who has missed the chance of an apprenticeship and is confined to unskilled work.

Jeremy's plan for a properly funded and high quality apprenticeship scheme will once again have FE colleges at its centre, a living wage that includes apprentices, and a ban on zero hours contracts. This is the start of recognising that our future roles, whatever they are and through whichever route, are of equal value.

Not all of us have a supportive parent to help navigate the complex maze of further education and higher education, and these are now businesses, so mistakes are costly. Therefore, Jeremy's proposal for a statutory youth service, giving advice and guidance, is an invaluable resource.

Family support services are bursting at the seams – Child and Adolescent Mental Health Services (CAMHS); Social Services. This morning, The employment agency Indeed advertised 387 social worker posts in the Nottingham area. Charities in our city, such as

Imara, working with children and young people who have been abused, have to manage increased referrals with reduced funding.

Holes are being cut in our safety net and we are slipping through, causing society to lose contributions from bright young people. Jeremy Corbyn is the only candidate with policies that seek to rectify the disproportionate effect of austerity on those most in need.

I'm one of many second generation immigrants and the climate of fear surrounding the immigration debate, ignited by the media and perpetuated by politicians, makes me wonder when they'll 'come for me'. I welcome Jeremy's unapologetic celebration of the benefits of immigration and the contributions we've made to Britain.

Young people are astutely principled but switched off from party politics, and is it any wonder? Westminster seems remote, disingenuous, and we feel screwed over by politicians who often don't consult, or represent our views.

Whilst canvassing, the familiar refrain from the young was that we would have voted if we understood politics more and if the parties were offering something worth voting for.

Jeremy Corbyn represents an honest politics that we can connect with, devoid of spin and pomposity. His campaign isn't even about him – he's the face of a wider movement that is inclusive and captivating. We no longer have to choose between young people and the elderly, schools and health care; we can all have a slice of the cake.

We've reached a critical juncture and how we vote in this leadership election will change the course of history. I've felt consumed by the momentum of this movement and I'm immensely privileged to be part of it. Under Jeremy Corbyn, the Labour Party will once again be the people's Party, for everyone in every workplace and every household.

PART 2

Campaign and Victory

4
#JEZWEDID

From Red Labour to Jeremy Corbyn
A tale from social media

Ben Sellers

Ancient History

I'm not seeking to give some sort of rounded, academic history of
the Jeremy Corbyn campaign. That will have to wait for another
day, when the actual work has been done and we're surveying from
the top of a hill marked 'Socialism in Our Lifetime'. For the
moment, I can only offer a partial glimpse of how the campaign was
constructed – and at that, only one aspect of it – the social media
campaign. Of course there are a thousand other strands. I don't
deny that, but this is the strand in which I was immersed for fourteen
weeks and, as it has been almost totally ignored by most of the
mainstream media, I think it's an important tale to tell. Of course,
one of the reasons why social media is ignored by the mainstream
is that there is often no single person to hang the story around.
Social media campaigning is mostly a collective, anonymous
enterprise – and where's the story in that?

The story has characters, though. It begins in 2011 with a simple
Facebook page, *Red Labour*, set up by Alex Craven – a Brighton-
based socialist in the Labour Party. Alex is someone who
recognised, at a very early stage, the power of Facebook to counter
the continued Blairite dominance in the Party. The *Red Labour* page
was initially set up in opposition to two colours of Labour which
had come to dominate the Parliamentary Party – as well as the think
tanks and party bureaucracy which buttressed the right of centre
bloc at Westminster. The first, and dominant faction was Purple
Labour, or 'Progress', as they tended to sell themselves. They were
the bearers of the New Labour flame, a well-oiled machine with
almost insurmountable power amongst the elected élite of the Party,
able to win parliamentary selections at a canter all over the country.

More recently, a new bloc had emerged, with nothing but a

collection of 'intellectuals', a load of media connections. and the odd MP. Blue Labour were closer to the old right of the Party, but had rebranded with some anti-immigrant rhetoric and strange intellectualisations of the traditions of the Party and the plight of the white working class. The key to Blue Labour's influence was their connections to the leader's office under Ed Miliband, rather than any pretence of building a movement, either within or without the Party. If they had, I doubt they would have given themselves the toxic name Blue Labour.

Red Labour was originally set up as a 'rapid rebuttal' to New Labour/One Nation Labour spin, which was a feature of both Purple and Blue Labour and the way they exercised their power. It chose the best contributions from Labour left social media activists, publicised critiques of the status quo, and displayed a hugely irreverent attitude to the grandees of the Party. It was funny, sharp and relentless in its pursuit of hypocrisy within the upper echelons of the Party. With its use of graphics and snappy, shareable content, it soon took off. At a time when people were just discovering the possibilities of 'mini blogs' on Facebook, the *Red Labour* page gained 10,000 followers in short time. Suddenly, the unashamed socialist left of the party had an audience.

At that point, in 2011, the situation of the traditional left of the party couldn't have been more different. Absolutely without influence, centred around the Labour Representation Committee (LRC) – the 'red' part of the Party had been marginalised by the concentration of power in the Parliamentary Labour Party. A small group of MPs still organised with the grassroots left of the Party, but they tended to be the equally marginalised Jeremy Corbyn and John McDonnell. There was a further problem. The Labour Representation Committee was failing to gain any real traction in the Party itself. The grassroots movement, which we all knew needed to be built, wasn't developing in the way we all knew it needed to if we were to mount a challenge. With the heavily resourced Progress still trouncing the left in selections, and Blue Labour whispering in Ed's ear, the LRC, for all their commitment, didn't look like breaking this vicious cycle.

A few younger LRC activists, including myself and Max Shanly, felt that we needed to take radical steps and joined Alex in pursuing the *Red Labour* project. A bit laughably, some of the more excitable sections of the left, positioned around the Labour Representation Committee, called it a 'split' when it was nothing of the sort. It was just that, like Alex, we believed there was a huge opportunity to connect to a whole group who were beyond the reach of those traditional approaches to socialist politics. Though, like many others, we had criticisms of the LRC, it wasn't fundamentally about that (I still have my LRC membership card), but we decided to target our efforts at building *Red Labour*. With more of us contributing, the page grew at a rapid pace. It became more creative, more diverse, and more focused on changing the Party. *Red Labour*, on Facebook at least, first became one of the liveliest spaces for the Labour left, and soon, at 20,000, the largest (with the exception of the official Labour Party page).

Inevitably, people soon started to talk about taking it offline. After a bit of deliberation, we decided to help people set up regional groups and the wider, more ambitious *Red Labour* project was starting to take shape, based not on a membership-style organisation, but a looser supporter network. This brought a whole new group of activists into the Red Labour operation. In about the space of a year (from 2012 to 2013) it had turned into a serious group within the party. We continued with our staples – we had a particular penchant for Nye Bevan memes, for instance – but now people were meeting offline and organising locally and regionally. That made us stronger, but with more of a sense of responsibility.

The point about *Red Labour* is that it was always seen as a serious intervention into the Party, but we weren't prepared to play by the rules which seemed to have been set out by those on the left and right of us. It wasn't quite so earnest as either – it was explicitly populist and accessible. As the 2015 election approached, for example, we presented a series of radical policy proposals, but in badge form. We sought out debate, sometimes controversy – and we tested things out, knowing we'd make mistakes occasionally. This was so radically different from the official output from the Party, that it continued to attract a following, both on Facebook and Twitter. Occasionally, we'd post things that the whole team wouldn't necessary agree with. The Scottish Referendum was a case in point. We didn't have unanimity within the group, so we decided to post both Yes and No articles on an equal basis.

At other times we'd pull posts as dissent became obvious within the organisers' group we'd assembled. Our attitude from day one was never to duck an issue. Let's argue it out – on the page, through the threads. The philosophy was that, on everything from migration to welfare, we needed to win hearts and minds, even if that meant engaging in late night (and sometimes tedious) battles on the *Red Labour* page. Gradually, we found that regular visitors to the page would take on each other, normally in a fairly comradely way, but our approach was always an interventionist one. This made it fraught at times, but through all that, we stuck together, determined that we could work together and build this project together – and aware that there weren't many chances left.

Pre-history

When Ed Miliband resigned in the immediate aftermath of that calamitous General Election, our *Red Labour* group was generally sceptical about the idea of running a candidate from the left. During the election campaign, we'd done some analysis of the strength of the left of the party in Parliament (and as candidates) and even with a small group of union-backed new candidates being elected, the prospects weren't good. We estimated 48/49 MPs who could be seen as either rebels or on the left of the party. Even this was stretching the meaning of both words to breaking point. We were fully aware that, as a result of the Collins Review, the bar for PLP nominations had been set even higher. The Parliamentary Party's veto was formidable. When Andy Burnham declared early and his team swooped on at least twenty of that list without so much as a blink of the eye, the prospects looked even bleaker. However, within the *Red Labour* group, the debate began – and we ran over the possibilities again and again. We wrote letters to some of the most likely suspects, even if it was just to put up a candidate so we could have a debate about the veto that the Parliamentary Party had over the choice of a leader.

At this point (in this no-mans-land between Ed resigning and the Labour left finding themselves a candidate) two important things happened which have been buried amongst all the other factors that have been cited. James Doran, a *Red Labour* organiser in Darlington, set up a Facebook page, 'We want John McDonnell as Labour Leader'. As we had contacted John already, we knew that he wasn't likely to stand again, but James decided to go ahead with the page, because if nothing else the group would serve as a pole of attraction for those who wanted a left candidate. That's exactly what happened – with an enormous amount of early interest. It was obvious that we weren't the only ones. Around 20 May 2015, two activists, Chelley Ryan and Beck Barnes, contacted us at the *Red Labour* page, saying that they were planning to write an open letter entitled 'We want an anti-austerity leader'. They asked if we'd look at it and Naomi Fearon, a member of our organising group, suggested a 38 Degrees petition. She worked on it with me and we collectively decided on the right wording. When Chelley and Beck launched it, the petition got an incredible response. It was shared via *Red Labour*, but Chelley and Beck – with Naomi's help – also did an incredible job attracting interest through a wide range of networks. Within a few days, 5,000 people had signed the petition and then, just as it was about to be sent off to John Cryer, the chair of the PLP, we heard the amazing news that Jeremy Corbyn had agreed to stand. We weren't sure how this had happened, but later we heard that it was, ironically, John McDonnell who had played the biggest part in persuading Jeremy.

The 'Little Win': The Nomination Campaign

We raised a few virtual glasses to toast Jeremy Corbyn that evening. When the news filtered through (I believe it was Diane Abbott who broke the news – through Twitter, of course), at first there was a sense of incredulity. For several weeks, we'd been desperately worried that the left would have no voice within the three-month race. We'd even looked into the possibility of organising, at Owen Jones' suggestion, 'not the leadership' rallies, which would discuss the alternatives to the 'austerity lite' narrative likely to be the theme of the leadership circus over the summer. When the news of Jeremy's candidature came through, then, it felt like our first victory. Even if nothing came of it, we had contributed to laying down a marker – that the socialist left in the Party hadn't been completely silenced.

The next morning I got a call from John McDonnell asking if I could co-ordinate the social media campaign to get Jeremy the nominations. Of course I agreed straight away – this was an incredible chance to play a small part in history. I discussed this with fellow Durham Red Labourite, Paul Simpson, and we set up a little campaign headquarters in the People's Bookshop in Durham and set to work on digging out articles, quotes and images of Jeremy. Both of us had cut our teeth with *Red Labour* and felt we understood the impact of really good, interactive and provocative social media content. Others across the country started helping out – Marsha Jane Thompson and Max Shanly down in London, Adam White in Manchester, and a host of others. We used the *Red Labour* page and our own contacts to kick start it, but the main thing was timing. The Facebook page and Twitter account went live within 12 hours of the announcement – and that was crucial. That enabled us to take maximum advantage of the coverage of Corbyn's surprise announcement and capitalise on the immediate surge in interest. Within 24 hours, we had a couple of thousand people on the page and had gained hundreds of followers on Twitter.

Once the initial building of the page and Twitter had been done, we determined to get to work on the MP nominations, one by one. *Red Labour* was a virtual campaign HQ. In amongst this burst of activity, we received a private message from a Labour councillor, which said simply #JezWeCan. He contacted us not long after asking us to not credit him with what we saw as a good pun at the time, and in the delay, another Red Labourite, Hazel Nolan, had tweeted the hashtag (apparently the very first to do so). We thought it was a good joke – a tongue in cheek reference to the Obama campaign slogan – but not for a second did we think it would become the political phrase of the summer. No matter, we posted a meme up on *Red Labour* with the #JezWeCan hashtag and a picture of Jeremy. That meme would later be turned into a t-shirt by Marsha Jane and a load of grassroots Unison activists at Scottish Unison Conference. It was an electrifying buzz to find the left suddenly alive with creativity.

But there was less sexy work to get on with, too. The *Red Labour* collective got to work preparing spreadsheets, we published email addresses and Twitter accounts, drew up lists and crossed names off the lists a matter of hours later. All the time, the possibilities were becoming narrower and narrower. Nevertheless, we carried on regardless – organising Twitter storms, petitions, and mass letter writing campaigns. Of course, we didn't realise how hard it would be, but a strange thing happened: the more resistant MPs seem to be, the more people seemed to want to get involved. People came out of nowhere and took responsibility for huge chunks of the campaign. At first, there was some apprehension – should we be taking a more centralised approach? But after deliberating for all of a few minutes, it became obvious that events had overtaken our plans – it was no longer 'our' campaign – it belonged to those who wanted to contribute. And this nominations campaign had become an issue of democracy.

The sum total of the online activity was just incredible – and relentless. This now was reaching far beyond our *Red Labour* group. Here came the 'Corbynistas'! Some people gave over whole evenings to emailing everyone on the list. Others engaged their own MPs in lengthy debates over twitter. It was a genuinely spontaneous and collective moment. It was an intense week of activity. While we were organising the mass emailing and tweeting of MPs, a thousand activist flowers were blooming. One of the most significant was Stuart Wheeler's change.com petition: 'We call on Labour MPs to nominate Jeremy Corbyn', which gained over 7,500 signatures after being extensively shared on social media and featured in the press. Stuart, from St Blazeys in the South West, was known to us in *Red Labour*, but again, his petition was a perfect example of someone just getting off their backside and deciding that they were going to give the campaign their all. We weren't going to bow down to the PLP and their accepted ways of doing things – the 'common sense' which said that they knew best who should be on the ballot paper and how the debate should be framed. There was a real sense in which we were determined to have our voice heard, at last. And we did. That's why, when the mainstream press decided that those nominations were 'gifted', it stuck in the craw. It wasn't true.

On that Monday lunchtime, 15 June 2015, we live tweeted the final hours of the nominations process. Sitting there, waiting for news from John McDonnell, refreshing the twitter account maniacally, was agony. I was personally quite confident that we'd done it – but I now realise that was partly wishful thinking: surely all that effort, everyone's efforts, couldn't have been in vain? Well, they could quite easily have been. There were some cat and mouse games being played, and as John later revealed, a couple of MPs were waiting outside the lobby, not wanting to be the 35th MP to nominate, until they were virtually dragged in by John. When he quickly announced on his Facebook page that the threshold had been passed, we revealed the incredible news to the social media world instantly. If it had been a football stadium, the place would have erupted, such was the reaction. I sat there and stared at my computer screen and I'm not ashamed to say that I seriously welled up as the enormity of what we had done hit home. The PLP nominations were a massive hurdle – we'd beaten their effective veto on party democracy.

The 'Big Win': The Leadership Election

So here we were. If getting a candidate was part one, and getting the nominations was part two, part three was the big one: how to get a 200-1 shot elected to the leadership of the Labour Party. This time, I took the initiative. I immediately contacted John and asked if I could carry on with the social media campaign role. It didn't take long to wrap up. I contacted my PhD supervisors, who were incredibly helpful, and I was granted a period of interruption in my studies to work on the campaign full time. The decision to give me licence to develop an independent social media campaign alongside Jeremy's personal social media accounts proved to be one of the best decisions of the campaign. I enlisted the help of Marsha Jane Thompson, who I knew mainly through the Labour Representation Committee, and we quickly assembled a small group of volunteers. Right from the off, this group gave the campaign a massive shot in the arm – it was a constantly vibrant, creative, enthusiastic and absolutely relentless campaign.

I'd argue, too, that this activity was the driver for much of the most positive aspects of the campaign: getting across Jeremy's central messages of respect and encouraging debate rather than a beauty contest; the popularisation of the policy interventions; pushing fundraising targets; and encouraging engagement as volunteers, supporters and attendance at the huge events all over the country. Most importantly, it was able to blunt some of the media attacks by relentlessly pushing a positive message and creating alternative sources of 'news' for our supporters. (In a recent YouGov survey, 57% of Corbyn supporters stated that they saw social media as their main source for news for the campaign, as opposed to 38-41% for other candidates and 32% for the wider population.)

I became more of a co-ordinator proper, asking the team to come up with memes, fishing out articles and quotes. In contrast to some of the other leadership campaigns, our social media campaign was completely organic and grassroots. We had assembled a team of activists around the left of the Party: people who could design those memes, who understood Jeremy's politics, and who were in touch with the wider movement. There was deliberately no thematic line. It was creative and, at times, *ad hoc*, but it connected with people much better than the slick offerings of the other candidates. We had a constant supply of fantastic contributions from Andrew Fisher and the central policy team, and, gradually – a load of good news stories – not from the mainstream press, but from the website team; from those out with Jeremy at hustings all over the country; the enormous rallies that followed; the amazing volunteer operation run by Kat Fletcher, and the massively professional phone bank operation co-ordinated by Alex Halligan.

This all fed into the next stage of the election campaign: the CLP nominations. This was being co-ordinated centrally via the 'ground operations team', but we used social media not only to raise awareness of the process, but also, crucially, to celebrate the successes. So when a CLP nominated Jeremy, they would get a little 'thank you' meme quickly produced by our design team. The response, especially on Twitter, was phenomenal. Throughout, the newly installed regional organisers, 12 strong, were running around, putting in the most incredible shifts to make sure we capitalised on this momentum and secured as many CLP nominations as possible – updating the regional Facebook pages when they could take time to draw breath. When the results started coming through, it was like an earthquake. This was so significant because we had expected to struggle amongst established party members. As those CLP nominations racked up, we realised that we'd underestimated our fellow party members. This was a genuine grassroots revival in the party. Of course, we could all claim we'd seen it coming and via *Red Labour* we'd always said it was possible but, nevertheless, this was incredible.

Organising ourselves around the phrase that would become emblematic of not just the social media campaign, but also the campaign as a whole: #JezWeCan, the social media team – which was split over four cities from London to Durham – worked together in absolute, collective unity, mostly via a single Facebook thread. Marsha Jane Thompson, my fellow co-ordinator, was a fantastic ally throughout – totally reliable, she also managed the online shop which produced the #JezWeCan t-shirts, raised a ton of cash for the campaign, and organised the huge Union Chapel fundraiser night in London. She carried the Twitter operation for much of the time, ably helped by James Doran in Darlington. I did most of my work from Durham, and when Marsha became officially part of the media strategy team down in London, the whole thing started really clicking. James did much of the Twitter grind of following accounts (even some which later proved not to be quite what they seemed at first sight). Paul Simpson, my colleague at the People's Bookshop, was one of the constants throughout who built the presence of the Facebook campaign at the crucial stage before nominations and was relentless in publicising Jeremy's proud history as a Member of Parliament.

Unison's Andrew Berry was our eyes and ears for stories on the ground. The incredibly talented Leonora Partington gave us the most fantastic, fearless graphics – some of which were shared to millions. At times we were firing this stuff out at a rate of knots, so the help of Ruth Berry and Charley Allan was crucial in rebutting the nasty and cynical attacks from the traditional media. Jason Harris was the campaign's brilliant photographer and captured both

Jeremy and our events superbly, which helped so much when it came to producing the shareable graphics. Yannis Mendez's videos were just brilliant – they really captured the diverse grassroots authenticity of the campaign and rightly received rapturous feedback. Finally, Jack Bond was the link between the social media team and the central campaign – a real team player who at one point drove through the night from London to deliver Durham Miners Gala leaflets, arriving at 3am. We worked so well together – with genuine respect, creativity and comradeship. Nobody even got upset over my pedantry about commas and colons.

The #JezWeCan social media campaign has been, by a long stretch, the biggest single campaign for an individual politician this country has ever seen. Sure, we had the raw material too. Jeremy was a dream candidate for the social media age: everything he said was clear, accessible and without jargon. Jeremy's record could speak for itself, but he'd never had such a platform. Our Facebook page gained nearly 70,000 likes in three months, with our top post reaching 750,000 people. On a weekly basis, between 1.5 and 2 million people were seeing our Facebook posts (immediately following the election win, it topped 6 million). In terms of engagement (likes, shares and comments), the average weekly engagement was around the 200k mark, with a peak of 600k in late July, with another peak just after the result of 800,000. 18,000 people signed up to go to our virtual Facebook event 'I'm voting for Jeremy Corbyn in the Labour leadership election'. Our output averaged about 10 posts a day, which over the three months will be close to 1,000 posts. On Twitter, we gained 64,000 followers, nearly 250,000 mentions were made of the campaign on Twitter, and our top tweet was retweeted 1,800 times. We posted a total of 4,100 tweets (including retweets). Our most successful Twitter storm saw the campaign mentioned 22,500 times in just two hours, but other Twitter 'events' saw our campaign trending at various times throughout the summer. At the last televised hustings in Gateshead, our campaign had 69% of all Twitter mentions, with Cooper and Burnham on 14%, and Liz Kendall on 3%. Our top embedded video was Owen Jones' speech at the Glasgow rally, with 97.1k views and a reach of 291,000. We have also experimented with Instagram, which has a much younger demographic and is focused on sharing images, gaining 1,430 followers in a quick time, more than ten times any other candidate.

That's the campaign in numbers, but it's about so much more than the numbers – it's about the democratic possibilities which are opened up by this new medium and this extensive reach. It gives us leverage where previously there was very little, and it has been the generator for the campaign on the ground throughout the summer. The extraordinary attendances at rallies were in part generated by the online campaign, which laid the foundations for the huge appetite for Jeremy's ideas and our policy discussions by making sure that Jeremy was constantly in the public eye, with quotes, selected highlights from articles, 'unity' statements, interviews, and some superb videos which highlighted the grassroots movement as it was being built. All of this generated its own alternative media – which counteracted much of the negativity and bile being poured out from the mainstream media. More than that, it generated a real sense that this was a movement everyone could be involved in, discuss, interact with, get answers from (we dealt with hundreds if not thousands of individual messages and enquiries to the Facebook and Twitter pages). If people felt like actors in this campaign, rather than 'consumers' of it, a large part of that was down to our social media operation.

This is a massive and significant sea change in the way we do our politics. When the overwhelming 59.5% vote came through on that historic Saturday at the QEII Conference Centre, we knew that hundreds of thousands were poised to celebrate on Facebook and Twitter. When the first round results were announced, a few audible gasps were heard in the hall, but not from the social media team. We released the #JezWeDid meme – and it was shared to half a million within the hour.

For me, social media now needs to be seen as an integral part of what happens next. Although we rightly have scepticism about the Obama Administration, there's no doubt that as a social media campaign, they are still the model (though we also have a new model now being created by Bernie Sanders' campaign). What the Obama campaign did was quite radical. They allocated equal resources to their social media operation as they did to their traditional press operation. I think we need to embrace this new, democratic medium and do the same. It's important to have articles in *The Guardian, The Independent,* to have positive news coverage wherever possible, but it won't be enough. If we are serious about winning in 2020, we need to engage in a mass education campaign, making our policy messages accessible and popular. We need to launch the biggest ever social media counter-narrative to the storm that is coming our way. We learnt important lessons over the three months and we ran a great social media campaign, but we've only scratched the surface. The social media campaign has been an incredible experience, not just for those involved officially, but for everyone who has made a contribution – small and big. But all of us know that it can be so much better, so much bigger, and so much more effective if we are bold enough to take up the challenge.

This article originally appeared at https://theworldturnedupside downne.wordpress.com/2015/09/27/jezwedid-from-red-labour-to-jeremy-corbyn-a-tale-from-social-media/

5
After the 2015 General Election
Chris Williamson

The origins of Labour's disastrous 2015 election defeat can be traced back to the untimely death of John Smith in 1994. It could even be argued that the seeds were sown almost 20 years earlier, on 11 February 1975, when Margaret Thatcher defeated Ted Heath to become the new Tory leader. Her election started the process of creating a new political consensus based on neoliberal economics. Friedrich Hayek and Milton Friedman became the new economic gurus, and the post-war Keynesian settlement, heralded by the 1945 Attlee-led Labour government and largely accepted by subsequent Tory prime ministers, was jettisoned by the Conservative Party.

The ideas of the New Right, seen as completely beyond the pale for more than three decades, came to dominate the Conservative Party's policy agenda, and ultimately influenced the thinking of the Labour Party, too.

Despite the fact that economic growth from 1945 to 1979 matched, if not outperformed, anything achieved in the next 36 years by the deregulated, financial-service-sector dominated economy, the conventional wisdom was that 'there was no alternative'.

By the time Tony Blair was elected Labour leader on 21 July 1994, the Party had suffered four successive, crushing election defeats at the hands of the Tories. He wasted no time in signalling his intention to take the Party in a different direction and used his conference speech later that year to call for Clause IV of the Labour Party's constitution to be abandoned. It was this clause that committed Labour to public ownership, but Blair wanted a totemic victory to announce the arrival of 'New Labour', devoid of ideological baggage, that he felt was hobbling the Party's electoral prospects. On 29 April 1995, a special conference was convened and members voted through the constitutional change that Blair craved. It was that decision that embedded the neoliberal consensus within the Labour Party.

Of course, Labour then went on to win three general elections in a row. Many New Labour luminaries therefore argued that it was essential to continue subscribing to this post-Keynesian neoliberal consensus in order to secure electoral success.

The electoral Holy Grail was the so-called 'middle ground', which Labour had to capture in order to win elections. But that meant acquiescing to policy assumptions that were previously seen as completely bonkers by virtually all serious commentators, and were anathema to the Labour Party from its foundation. Consequently, the policy agenda of Labour governments from 1997 to 2010 did very little to tackle the hegemony of the financial services industry. The City continued to dominate, and Labour ministers were bedazzled by this cash cow that generated significant tax revenues, which were used for Labour's investment in public services.

But the cash cow grazed on unsafe ground and, when the financial crash arrived, the Labour government was overly exposed. Tax revenues diminished, and public expenditure dramatically increased to save the banks from a complete meltdown. The Tories and their friends in the media used this calamity to change the terms of debate. Until then, George Osborne and David Cameron were committed to matching Labour's spending plans, but this presented them with the perfect opportunity to reveal their true, fundamentalist Thatcherite colours.

Suddenly, according to the Tories and their chums in the media, the country's economic woes were all the fault of a profligate Labour government lavishing public money on incompetent public services and lazy welfare scroungers. The fact that Labour's economic and social policies had been influenced by a neoliberal doctrine, and that most of the underlying changes Margaret Thatcher had foisted on the country remained in place, was discounted. Most cynical of all was that the origins of the financial crash – the 1986 deregulation of the City, for which Mrs Thatcher's government was responsible – were conveniently forgotten; as was the deindustrialisation of Britain's economy for which her government was also responsible. This exponentially compounded matters when the banking collapse occurred.

The financial meltdown presented an opportunity for the Tories to create a narrative that Labour's profligacy caused the crash, and this was used relentlessly up to the 2010 election and throughout the last parliament. It was then rolled out again for the 2015 general election campaign.

The problem for the Labour Party was that it did not have a credible counterbalancing story to tell. Ed Balls insisted that people needed '*to trust us to make difficult decisions*'. Ed Miliband said the '*hard reality*' was that he wouldn't '*be able to promise to reverse*' Tory cuts if Labour won in 2015. Public sector workers were told by Labour that they would have to accept a derisory one per cent pay cap.

Labour had effectively surrendered to the neoliberal consensus 20 years ago, so it allowed the Tories to set the agenda on economic and public policy in the 2010 and 2015 campaigns. Every time a Shadow Cabinet member was interviewed, they were asked how much they would cut in order to demonstrate Labour's fiscal credibility, which invariably left them floundering in search of a convincing reply. There was no convincing reply, because Labour's capitulation to neoliberalism two decades earlier was firmly embedded in the policy outlook of the Shadow front bench.

During the Blair-Brown years, there was an abject failure to rebalance the economy. Companies were allowed to continue offshoring well-paid and skilled jobs, emerging green technologies were given inadequate support, and public procurement policies saw huge manufacturing contracts going overseas. Privatisation continued apace, resulting in large tracts of public service provision being run by private companies, whose primary purpose was private profit rather than public service. Profit margins were enhanced by squeezing the terms and conditions of privatised workforces, and the quality of service provided was invariably diminished. The New Labour mantra that allowed this to continue was 'what matters is what works'.

Tony Blair and his New Labour cabinet ministers were obsessed with what he described as public service reform, which invariably meant giving the private sector an increasing input into public services. Private Finance Initiatives (PFI) became the norm for public sector investment. Local authorities had to establish public-private partnerships and create special purpose vehicles to get anything done.

Regional development agencies, regeneration companies, academy schools and hospital trusts were created, and all had to be led by the business community. It was a continuation of the Tory philosophy of 'private good, public bad', which had the effect of alienating many dedicated public servants.

After Ed Miliband was elected Labour leader in 2010, on a wave of optimism that he would lead a radical overhaul of Labour's policy agenda, the ensuing four-and-a-half years were a big disappointment. Hopes were dashed of clear proposals on totemic issues such as bringing the railways back into public ownership, a renaissance in council housing, bringing academies within the orbit of local authorities, and offering a plausible alternative to austerity.

Pleas from Labour Party members, to stop the fragmentation of our education service, to give local authorities the resources needed to deliver essential services, and to support a compassionate social security system, also fell on stony ground.

Ed Miliband's progressive instincts, that he displayed during his successful leadership election campaign, never really materialised. The early signs were positive though, with Jon Cruddas appointed to lead a radical policy overhaul. Cruddas's extensive work was largely ignored. Instead, the public were offered a series of ideas that were neither fish nor fowl. For example, rather than giving a clear, unambiguous commitment to take the train operating companies back into public ownership when the franchises came up for renewal, a convoluted plan was offered in its place. Labour's proposal was to establish a public sector operator to bid for the franchises against the private train-operating companies. Such a scheme would have been incredibly bureaucratic, expensive to run, and offered no guarantee that it would win the contracts.

The Manifesto was full of such tortuous compromises, which meant Labour's message was confused and lacked ambition, resulting in people being unclear about what Labour really stood for. Consequently, in the 2015 election the Labour Party was outflanked by the UK Independence Party (UKIP), the Green Party and Plaid Cymru, in England and Wales, and by the Scottish National Party (SNP) in Scotland.

There were, of course, plenty of good things in the Labour Manifesto, such as the pledges to end exploitative zero hours contracts, abolish the pernicious bedroom tax, and stop the privatisation of the NHS. But there was no clear narrative – no big idea. This meant that the good things in the Manifesto were drowned out by the Party's failure to demonstrate economic credibility. The Tories set the terms of debate on the economy because Labour was still hidebound by neoliberalism, and the resultant commitment to austerity that such an obsession requires.

The much trumpeted four million doorstep conversations Labour activists had with voters, that Douglas Alexander, Labour's campaign coordinator, was so pleased about, were therefore not as effective as they could have been. A YouGov poll in January 2015 found a majority of the public were more likely to vote Labour if the party rejected austerity and offered a more positive alternative instead[1]. The poll was undertaken after 15 Labour MPs published a statement that same month calling on the party to adopt an alternative to continued austerity and spending cuts until 2019-20[2].

These appeals for a more progressive and hopeful vision were disregarded in favour of the tried and tested approach that, it was claimed, had brought massive electoral success in 1997, 2001 and 2005. This was done in spite of the fact that 2010 had suggested people now wanted something different. The fact that Labour had lost four million votes, compared to the high point in 1997, didn't appear to register with the Party hierarchy, who seemed to place blind faith in the old formula.

Ed Miliband won the Labour leadership on a platform of 'turning the page on New Labour', but he didn't follow through on his commitment. The New Labour ethos ran through the approach taken by Ed and his shadow cabinet like letters through a stick of rock.

The electorate demonstrated their disapproval of New Labour in 2010 and, by the time of the 2015 general election, there was no apparent appetite for a Labour Party obsessed by triangulation and sound bites. People were yearning for a fresh approach.

This failure to inspire and provide a clear alternative led directly to Labour's poor showing in the polls in the 2015 general election. There were 15.6 million people who didn't bother voting for anyone, while 3.8 million voted for UKIP, 1.5 million supported the SNP, and 1.1 million backed the Green Party. Furthermore, nearly a million people didn't even make it onto the register, a problem that was exacerbated by the partial implementation of the new Individual Electoral Registration system. This is a problem that could be even worse by the time of the next election when Individual Electoral Registration is fully implemented.

Party organisers were given an almost impossible task by a Manifesto that didn't sufficiently differentiate the Party and lacked any convincing or appealing thread knitting it all together. The very first page was devoted to the so-called 'Budget Responsibility Lock' in an attempt to convince a sceptical electorate that Labour would better manage an inherently unfair economic system. People have seen how this economic system has permitted inequality to flourish.

Instead of taking the Tories to task for presiding over a grotesque increase in poverty and inequality, Labour stuck to the line about fiscal credibility requiring the Party to continue to make cuts. To paraphrase, the Party's message was '*look, it's going to be tough under a Labour government; it just won't be quite as tough as it is under the Tories*'. Throughout the short campaign, Labour was constantly kept on the back foot because of the timidity of its offer. That timidity was driven by its unwillingness or its inability to throw off the yoke of neoliberalism that Tony Blair had placed around the Party's neck in 1995. This prevented Labour from offering a distinctive vision, and resulted in the party haemorrhaging votes to UKIP, the SNP and the Green Party. Votes lost to the Green Party alone allowed the Tories to secure an overall majority. Votes lost to the SNP saw Labour all but wiped out in Scotland. And votes lost to UKIP gifted the Tories a whole bunch of seats that Labour should have won.

There were 10 Labour-Tory marginal seats where the Green Party obtained more votes than the majority achieved by the successful Tory candidate. Had Labour offered a more progressive prospectus, or even if it had emphasised the positive policy areas that were included in the 2015 Manifesto, the outcome might have been very different. Those seats would have been won by Labour, the Tories would have been eight short of an overall majority, and the election aftermath would have been completely different.

What happened next

Nobody could have predicted what happened next. After Ed Miliband resigned it looked like business as usual, with all the early frontrunners to replace him offering pretty much the same thing. The exchanges that took place in the Labour leadership race were a pretty lacklustre affair. It was failing to excite existing Party members, let alone arouse much interest from the wider general public, other than passing curiosity. The Labour Party was in a state of collective depression, which it didn't look like recovering from any time soon. That was until the eleventh hour candidature of Jeremy Corbyn, which instantaneously electrified a dreary, uninspiring contest between candidates who, to varying degrees, had accepted the Tories' austerity scam.

When Jeremy announced he was standing, it wasn't clear that he would even secure enough MP nominations to make it on to the ballot paper. Yet, when he did, many people thought he would be lucky to come third and, in all probability, would be fourth, behind the other three '*sensible*' and '*mainstream*' candidates. His supporters consoled themselves with the hope that Jeremy would achieve a 'respectable vote' and wouldn't be humiliated. But things really took off and, suddenly, it looked like Jeremy was going to do better than expected; then he was challenging to be the frontrunner; and then he was the odds-on favourite to win.

This dramatic turn of events unleashed one of the most vituperative attacks on a leadership candidate for a political party that the UK has ever witnessed. It was probably worse than the hysteria surrounding Tony Benn's unsuccessful bid to become the deputy leader of the Labour Party, in 1981. Much of the media, the Conservatives, and various Labour luminaries were predicting electoral annihilation if Labour members were 'stupid' enough to elect this leftwing backbench maverick. But the more Jeremy was smeared, the more people rallied to his cause, and the more he was criticised the more people joined or became registered supporters of the Labour Party. The country was witnessing a phenomenon not seen in UK political history.

It became obvious that the combined, pent-up frustrations of hundreds of thousands of people were being exorcised by the policy agenda that Jeremy Corbyn was advocating. The public clearly liked his mild mannered but determined approach. People also respected his steadfast refusal to indulge in personal attacks. Despite intense provocation, he continued to say he was going to concentrate on the issues.

Verbal assaults from the right-wing media and political opponents in other parties were expected. What wasn't anticipated, perhaps, was the ferocity and absurdity of the criticisms from some senior figures inside the Labour Party. The consensus among those internal critics opposing Jeremy Corbyn's policy prospectus was that Labour must accept that cuts have to be made in order to regain the trust of the electorate. But their strictures seemed to ignore the opinion of some of the world's leading economists, who argue that austerity is the problem and not the solution.

Nobel Prize-winning economist, Paul Krugman, is one of those who has spoken out against the austerity fallacy. Earlier in 2015, he wrote that the case for cuts was a 'lie' and said he didn't understand why some in Britain still believed it. Yet a number of Labour luminaries were happy to perpetuate this 'lie' to undermine Jeremy Corbyn's leadership election campaign. It seems they were caught in a neoliberal time warp.

According to Krugman: '*it's foolish and destructive to worry about deficits when borrowing is very cheap and the funds you borrow would otherwise go to waste*'. Although Jeremy Corbyn wasn't arguing for the government to permanently run big budget deficits, his proposal to reject austerity and invest in the economy was reinforced by Krugman's statement.

One of the more bizarre criticisms levelled against Jeremy Corbyn, by one prominent opponent, was that under his leadership the Labour Party would be in '*danger*' of becoming a '*populist anti-austerity movement*'. Given that austerity doesn't work, and the Oxford English Dictionary definition of '*populist*' is '*seeking to represent the interests of ordinary people*', being a populist anti-austerity movement was precisely what most people believed the Labour Party should be.

During the course of the Labour leadership race, Jeremy Corbyn spoke at 100 packed rallies, with the final one held in his own constituency of Islington North. The crowds flocking to these meetings were so large that most of the venues weren't big enough to accommodate them all. The political establishment inside and outside the Labour Party were completely disconcerted by this turn of events. They couldn't quite believe that the British public wanted to listen to this entirely different political prospectus, compared to the worn-out, old approach that had been served up over the previous twenty years. The political élite couldn't figure out why people actually had an appetite for socialist solutions to the country's problems. They thought socialism had been consigned to the history books; something to read about from a quaint bygone age – not something that would gain any traction in the modern era, let alone provide a platform on which to build a programme to win the leadership of the modern Labour Party. How wrong they were.

In September 2015, from being the rank outsider three months earlier, Jeremy won a landslide victory, securing 59.5 per cent of the vote. His closest rival was 40.5 per cent behind him. The full results show the scale of his overwhelming victory.

CORBYN	251,417	59.5%
BURNHAM	80,462	19.0%
COOPER	71,928	17.0%
KENDALL	18,857	4.5%

How did Corbyn do it?

This was a campaign that came from nowhere and secured the biggest mandate any British party political leader has ever achieved in internal elections. One of the most delicious ironies of Jeremy Corbyn's success is that the system by which he was elected was demanded by so-called Labour 'modernisers' to undermine the influence of trade unions on the outcome of leadership elections. A number of trade union leaders had cautioned the advocates of this new procedure to be careful what they wished for.

When it became obvious that Jeremy Corbyn was the candidate to beat, those self-same advocates cried foul. They called for the process to be suspended because much of the huge increase in registered supporters must be down to infiltration by far left groups and Conservative Party activists.

The Labour Party's bureaucracy was given the task of weeding out these disruptive interlopers to secure the integrity of the vote. But, with around 400,000 people signing up to take part in the election in just two months, the claims of mass infiltration were palpably absurd.

Even if every member of the Conservative Party and every single person associated with a far left group in Britain had joined, it would still have left around 250,000 new supporters unaccounted for. In the end, around 3,000 people were barred from voting, despite the fact that Labour Party staffers were forced to implement a process that was reminiscent of a cross between a Stasi interrogation and a McCarthyite witch-hunt.

It soon became clear that this was less about weeding out fifth columnists than a concerted effort to block supporters of Jeremy Corbyn. It led to ludicrous spectacles – trade union leader Mark Serwotka, legendary film maker Ken Loach, and leftwing comedian Mark Steel received letters saying they were disqualified from voting because they did not share Labour's values! Even Jeremy Corbyn's own brother was barred. But, despite the best endeavours of some in the Labour Party's hierarchy, the surge was so strong it was impossible to withstand the outpouring of support for Jeremy Corbyn's policy programme.

The so-called 'modernisers' were crestfallen after being hoist with their own petard. One such disconsolate 'moderniser' was Dan Hodges, who used his *Daily Telegraph* column for cathartic therapy. He self-flagellated his way through his column (14 August 2015) bemoaning that it was 'Progmods' (progressive modernisers) like himself, as he styled them, who were responsible. Although there was still a month to go before polls closed when he wrote that column, Hodges could see the writing on the wall. He concluded his *mea culpa* by saying:

' … if [Jeremy Corbyn] isn't stopped, then we know who to blame. Not Paul Kenny, [GMB general secretary] *or Dave Prentis,* [Unison general secretary] *or Len McCluskey* [Unite general secretary]. *The Left's progressive modernisers have to look at the self-satisfied reflections in the mirror. And the finger pointing directly at ourselves.'*

Jeremy Corbyn had come through the sternest of tests with flying colours. Every dirty trick in the book had been thrown at him. Former prime ministers and cabinet members were wheeled out to demand that people should not vote for him. The press and broadcast media had indulged in a campaign of vilification to demonise him. But none of it worked because his integrity shone through and his policy agenda was honest, refreshing and new. He appealed to everyone who believed the Labour Party should be a force for good and an agent for progressive change. In short they wanted Labour to be a party that would take on the corporate vested interests and super-rich oligarchs who have been getting even richer at the expense of everyone else in the country. They wanted a party that would reject austerity in favour of growing the economy and investing in public services. And they wanted a party that would listen to its members and reintroduce greater democracy into its policy making process.

That is why Jeremy Corbyn's leadership rallies were full to overflowing; why hundreds of thousands of people signed up to be part of the Labour Party. People wanted something different; something authentic; something that resonated with their experiences. They wanted a leader who they could believe in; who could empathise with them; fight their corner; and speak truth to power.

Jeremy carries the hopes, dreams and expectations of millions on his shoulders, but he will not be able to deliver all this on his own. The mass movement that the Labour Party is becoming will be crucial to the success of his leadership.

The enthusiastic supporters who helped secure Jeremy's stunning triumph showed how a campaign can successfully come through against all the odds. It was the dedication of these unsung heroes that carried Jeremy to victory. Their innovative organisational acumen cannot be overstated. The policy consultation documents, public meetings, constituency nomination hustings, and social media presence built an unstoppable momentum. These techniques will be invaluable for the Labour Party in campaigning to beat the Conservatives and other political opponents in future election campaigns.

The Future

With a majority in the House of Commons, the Conservatives intend to do everything in their power to make the 2020 election more difficult for Labour to win. The two biggest obstacles will be the proposal to reduce the number of parliamentary constituencies from six hundred and fifty to six hundred and the full rollout of the Individual Electoral Registration system.

Had the Tories managed to push through legislation in the last parliament to reduce the number of constituencies, psephologists suggest their majority could have been as high as forty-four following the 2015 election. As it turned out, they secured a majority of just twelve.

The partial rollout of the Individual Electoral Registration scheme prior to that election saw nearly a million voters drop off the register, which cost Labour dearly. Had the electoral register been drawn up in the same way as it was for the 2010 election, it is almost certain that the Conservatives would have been denied an overall majority.

However, the situation is set to get much worse. It has been estimated that up to seven million voters could fall off the register when Individual Electoral Registration is fully implemented. The Government has already been criticised by the Electoral Commission which said, in a press release issued on 16 July 2015, that it was 'disappointed' by the Government's plan to bring forward the end of the transition to Individual Electoral Registration.

Consequently, one of the most important tasks for the Labour Party and other sympathetic groups will be to engage in a mass voter registration exercise. Failure to do this successfully will make it even more difficult to dislodge the Tories in 2020. But, as challenging as this task might appear, it will be a walk in the park compared to the obstacles encountered by the US civil rights movement in the 1950s and 60s. Labour campaigners, involved in UK voter registration exercises, will not be subjected to the violence and intimidation meted out to those US civil rights activists. Anyone involved in the voter registration effort up to 2020 should therefore take inspiration from the heroic endeavours of their US civil rights counterparts from over half a century ago.

The Labour Party should also look at the success of the Conservative Party's 2015 election campaign and how it confounded the opinion pollsters, who all predicted a hung parliament. Nobody, save perhaps Lynton Crosby and his inner circle, believed the Tories would win an outright majority. Even the exit poll, watched in disbelief by everyone hoping for a Labour victory, did not predict a Conservative majority government.

What was it that Lynton Crosby did to confound all the psephological experts? A book by Tim Ross, published in October 2015, entitled: '*Why the Tories Won: The Inside Story of the 2015 Election*', provides a helpful insight. Reviewing it in *The Independent* (17 October 2015), columnist John Rentoul said Lynton Crosby had told him in March that he could '*see 23 seats we can win. We're on 303 at the moment.*'

What Crosby did successfully was to focus on direct mail, Facebook, and email, rather than on Twitter and YouTube. While Labour activists were busy having 'four million conversations' on the doorstep, the Tory Party was working away below the radar. The Conservative Party, with its much smaller and older membership, cannot match Labour's on-street presence, but its operation was far more sophisticated, ruthless and targeted.

Crosby is renowned for his dirty tricks and they were deployed to devastating effect against Ed Miliband and the Labour Party. He went through various iterations, depicting Ed Miliband as a dangerous left-winger, to a pathetic, incompetent fool who couldn't eat a bacon sandwich with dignity, let alone stand up to Nicola Sturgeon or Vladimir Putin. Meanwhile, Ed Balls was presented as the man responsible for driving the economy into the ditch and couldn't be trusted with the keys to the car again.

Of course, these depictions were made easier by the right-wing gutter press and a compliant broadcast media. But they do point to the pitiless misrepresentations to which Jeremy Corbyn and the Labour leadership team will be subjected right up to the general election in 2020, at the end of the five-year, fixed-term parliament. People have already had a preview of what will be served, but that has been a mere entrée to the main course of vilification yet to come, which will get worse and more intense.

The Conservative Party has access to virtually unlimited funds, which will roll in even more speedily if Labour, under Jeremy Corbyn, looks like beating the Tories. There are no depths to which they will not stoop to stop Jeremy Corbyn getting the keys to Number 10. They know their cosseted lifestyle and unaccountable power depends on the continuation of the neoliberal status quo. The last thing they want is a Labour Government committed to tax justice, reversing the privatisation of public services, and ending the monopolisation of the media by a handful of wealthy tax exiles.

So the task confronting Jeremy Corbyn's Labour Party is massive. It isn't made any easier by the handful of *refuseniks* and malcontents in the Parliamentary Labour Party whose presence has been grossly exaggerated by the media.

Nevertheless, the 2020 election is there for the taking. The unparalleled growth in the Labour Party's membership has made it a mass movement again and that will be a powerful counterbalance to a hostile media and a well-financed Tory Party campaign machine. But it will require the Labour Party matching what Tim Ross and John Rentoul described as the '*evidence-driven, disciplined, hard working and team spirited*' approach that Lynton Crosby's campaign team possessed.

Many lessons have been learned, not just by the Tory Party's success in the election but also by Jeremy Corbyn's victory too. His success was also down to an '*evidence-driven, disciplined, hard working and team spirited*' approach that saw him sweep to victory.

A Labour campaign committed to the agenda Jeremy Corbyn put forward in his leadership bid has the advantage over the Conservatives that Labour is on the side of ordinary people. No matter how hard Messrs Cameron and Osborne and their friends in the media try to rebrand the Conservative Party as the '*workers party*', they will never succeed. People know who the Tories represent and it certainly isn't workers.

Moreover, Labour's credibility on the economy has been enhanced by taking a distinctly anti-austerity stance. John McDonnell's ability to attract some of the world's best economists to his advisory panel highlights what a consummate shadow chancellor he is proving to be. The panel comprises:

Thomas Piketty, Professor, Paris School of Economics, author of the bestselling *Capital in the Twenty-First Century*

Joe Stiglitz, Professor, Columbia University, recipient of the 2001 Nobel Memorial Prize in economics

Mariana Mazzucato, Professor, University of Sussex

Anastasia Nesvetailova, Professor, City University London

Danny Blanchflower, Professor of Economics, Dartmouth College, USA, University of Stirling, former member of the Monetary Policy Committee

Ann Pettifor, Director of Policy Research in Macroeconomics (PRIME), and an Honorary Research Fellow at the Political Economy Research Centre of City University

In announcing these appointments, Jeremy Corbyn said:

> '*I was elected on a clear mandate to oppose austerity and to set out an economic strategy based on investment in skills, jobs and infrastructure. Our economy must deliver security for all, not just riches for a few.*'

This one decision to assemble an esteemed panel of experts will help rehabilitate Labour's reputation for economic trustworthiness. The phrase coined by Thomas Piketty that '*capitalism should be the slave of democracy, not the other way around*' should be used to underpin Labour's new approach to the economy. Piketty, Stiglitz and Pettifor *et al* will provide the rigour underpinning Labour's determination to make the economy work for ordinary people, not just the rich élite.

By setting out a distinctively Labour agenda the Party could win back people who have deserted it for the Greens, UKIP and the SNP. It could also mobilise people to the Labour cause who have previously given up on politics altogether. Anecdotal evidence from around the country suggests that people are impressed by the straight talking, honest politics that Jeremy Corbyn epitomises, and that includes some Tory voters, too, who could be won over.

Polling evidence shows that Jeremy Corbyn's policy agenda is popular with the electorate. A Labour programme promising to scrap tuition fees; regulate rents; build council houses; invest in infrastructure; close tax havens; nationalise the railways; bring the utilities under democratic control; introduce a statutory living wage; expand manufacturing; take academies and free schools into the orbit of local education authorities; establish a national investment bank; and reverse the attacks on our public services, underpinned by a coherent anti-austerity narrative, would be alluring to millions. It would give activists on the streets, candidates at public meetings, and spokespeople in TV and radio studios an attractive and positive narrative, unencumbered by tortuous triangulation. It would help to truly inspire people to vote Labour to transform the United Kingdom for generations to come.

Put like that, it all sounds relatively straightforward, but there is a lot of work to do over the next few years. The policy agenda needs to be formally agreed by the Party and there will be some difficult issues to come to terms with. The Parliamentary Labour Party needs to come together to put the Party's collective interests and the interests of the country before their own personal agendas. The handful of disgruntled MPs need to be brought onside and if they won't co-operate, they must not be allowed to derail the different politics that members and the country at large crave.

The Labour Movement needs to be engaged to participate in agreeing and then disseminating the policy agenda to the wider general public and to counter the negative media onslaught. That will mean having millions of meaningful conversations on the doorstep, in the workplace, within the family, and in community groups and networks. The conversations have to be genuinely meaningful, too, unlike those four million conversations Douglas Alexander boasted about prior to the last election. Those conversations were more about voter ID than actually having a two-way conversation with people.

Social media will play an increasingly important role, but it is not a panacea. Personal face-to-face contact is better, and ensuring that people see the Labour Party as integral to the community, not separate from it. With the Labour Party's membership growing rapidly, this will be an easier task to accomplish. The Labour Movement is embarking on a mammoth assignment and, as more individuals are inspired to get involved, the load will be shared among more and more people.

The prospect of Labour restoring its position in the vanguard of a British progressive movement is becoming a reality. This historic opportunity for Labour to lead a populist anti-austerity movement could sweep it back to power in 2020, installing Jeremy Corbyn as Prime Minister. Before the 2015 general election, such a proposition would have been dismissed as an impossible fantasy and nothing to do with *realpolitik*. But the fantasy becomes a distinct possibility. The awakening surge in Britain has the potential to turn into an inexorable tide.

If the Labour Movement rediscovers the spirit of 1945 and once again reaches out to build a coalition of interests, a new progressive consensus in the country could be born. Labour's mission is perhaps best summed up by the last verse of Percy Shelley's poem '*The Masque of Anarchy*', written almost 200 years ago in the aftermath of the Peterloo massacre.

> *Rise like Lions after slumber*
> *In unvanquishable number,*
> *Shake your chains to earth like dew*
> *Which in sleep had fallen on you—*
> *Ye are many—they are few.*

The prize of a new progressive consensus is there for the taking; with solidarity and in unity that prize can be claimed in 2020, and the first chapter of a new progressive period in British history is being written right now.

Notes
1. see http://tinyurl.com/q7ynnv7
2. see http://tinyurl.com/oz5tra5

6

Labour's Rules
The changes we've had and the changes we need
Christine Shawcroft

After the disappointments of the Wilson/Callaghan era, when Labour majorities were squandered, Annual Conference decisions ignored, and a cuts programme instituted which paved the way for Margaret Thatcher's monetarist mania, in the 1980s there was a huge campaign amongst Labour activists for greater accountability of individual Members of Parliament and the Leader of the Party. Until then, the Leader had been elected solely by members of the Parliamentary Labour Party (PLP).

Some of those MPs themselves had 'jobs for life': once they had been selected, as long as they held their seats, they could not be removed. This democratic deficit had led to a PLP and Leadership that was completely divorced from the rank and file Party membership.

Working with the trade unions and Constituency Labour Parties, the Campaign for Labour Party Democracy (CLPD) and others organised to get rule changes passed through Annual Conference which provided for mandatory reselection of sitting MPs, something which had long applied to local councillors without causing controversy, and to get agreed a new process of electing Labour leaders – the 'electoral college' of one-third MPs, one-third trade unions, and one-third individual members.

During the late seventies and early eighties, a large surge of young, left-wing activists joined the Labour Party and transformed what were often moribund local Parties. Some would-be members, in fact, were told they couldn't join the local Party because it was 'full', but eventually they forced their way in. The newly invigorated General Committees (GCs) proceeded to select left Parliamentary candidates, such as Alan Simpson, Dave Nellist, Dianne Abbott and, of course, Jeremy Corbyn. These GCs were made up of delegates from constituency branches, local trade union branches, and affiliated organisations such as the Co-operative Party and socialist societies. Leaders from Neil Kinnock onwards believed that, if left-wing activists on the GCs could be outflanked by the silent majority of right-wing members, all would be well.

Leader from 1992, John Smith, aided and abetted by John Prescott, brought in one member, one vote (OMOV) selections for Parliamentary candidates, although the make-up of the Parliamentary Labour Party wasn't substantially altered until the Blairite practice of parachuting in favoured candidates became commonplace. In 2010, the knife-edge election of Ed Miliband under a modified electoral college caused a great deal of ill will, although most of it was from the 'we-was-robbed' tendency around heir-to-Blair, David Miliband. Losing to David in the members' and MPs' sections, Ed won because of trade union votes. After earlier concerns about unions either not balloting their members, or about them balloting and then casting a block vote for the winner, regardless of how many votes the losing candidates got, the unions had balloted and then cast their votes proportionally to how many votes the candidates received in the ballots. Doubts about the legitimacy of Ed's victory were circulating from the beginning, and he was routinely accused of being in the pocket of trade union leaders.

In order to prove that he wasn't somehow under the control of trade unions, Miliband began attacking his erstwhile supporters. It had always been one of Blair's dreams to disaffiliate the trade unions from the Labour Party (as well as removing all power from rank and file members and founding a Progressive Party, in alliance with the Liberal Democrats, based on powerless 'supporters' only, along the lines of the American Democrats).

Blair, whilst Prime Minister from 1997 to 2007, had set up an inquiry into political party funding, which was supposedly to examine the dodgy millions pouring into Conservative Party coffers. Taking almost no notice of that, Lord Hayden Phillips immediately turned his attention to trade union affiliation to the Labour Party, and began proposing a cap on donations to parties which was clearly intended to cut off the major source of Labour funding. If the level of affiliation of trade unions was cut, their voting strength at Annual Conference would also be cut.

Ed Miliband let it be known that he was looking for a way to cut the link between trade unions and the Labour Party. When appointing a new General Secretary of the party, he had favoured Chris Lennie on the basis that Lennie had promised him that he would disaffiliate the unions, only to have the National Executive Committee vote against his tacit recommendation by selecting Iain McNicol. Just as it seemed the democratic waters were going to close over Miliband's head, he was able to clutch the straw of the Falkirk parliamentary selection.

All sorts of allegations of trade union manipulation of the selection process in Falkirk were made; none of them were subsequently discovered to be true. The long-suffering local party had had Eric Joyce imposed upon them in the first place, and were determined that this time they would select a candidate that they actually wanted, free from Head Office interference. To this end, Unite was signing up its members to be local party members, totally in accordance with the Rules of both bodies. Miliband pounced on the allegations, referred them to the police, although there was no evidence whatsoever of any criminal activity, and announced the setting up of the Collins Review.

Ray Collins (ennobled by then to Lord Collins) was a former General Secretary of the Party. Coming from a long line of right-wing General Secretaries, he was already strongly in favour of cutting the trade union link and bringing in a form of one member one vote for leadership elections. OMOV has been a right wing shibboleth since David Owen's 'Gang of Four' left the Labour Party and set up the Social Democratic Party (SDP) on this pretext, and successive leaders had seen it as the perfect way to bypass the delegate structure of the Labour Party, in favour of a supposedly more docile, more right-wing, majority of members.

The Collins Report proposed having an 'opt-in' system for trade union members who paid the political levy to say they support the Party's aims and values and thus become 'affiliated members'. After a lead-in time of five years, trade unions would have their affiliation cut to the number of their members who had not merely paid the political levy, but who had also signed up to become affiliated supporters. At the time, many trade union general secretaries forecast that only about ten per cent of their levy payers would sign up as affiliated members, which would reduce their affiliation to that figure, cutting their influence at Annual Conference and depriving the Labour Party of an estimated £7 million each year. Effectively, they would be disaffiliated from the Labour Party.

Interestingly, the current Tory Government has included this proposal of an opt-in for workers to join trade unions in the Trade Union Bill 2015. Whether they got the idea from Ray Collins, or he got the idea from them, no one is quite sure.

The Collins Report also came up with the idea of reinvigorating the system of registered supporters. This was dreamed up by Ed Miliband in a previous wave of 'reforms'. Supporters were to be signed up by some mysterious process known to no one, paid nothing and, once there were fifty thousand of them, they would be allowed a vote in any Party Leadership election. Collins proposed starting from scratch and having new registered supporters who would pay £3 and, in London, immediately get a vote in the proposed primary for London Mayoral candidate. Nationwide, they would get a vote in a Leadership election, should there be one. Much was made of the system used in France for the selection of the Socialist Party's Presidential candidate. Right-wingers in the Labour Party believed that a similar system, if used here, would transform a Leadership election. In this they were not mistaken. However, at the time (spring 2014), the Labour Party Left in general, and CLPD in particular, were extremely concerned about the Collins proposals, not least their drastic effect on Party finances. We were also concerned about the planned reduction in voting strength of the trade unions at Annual Conference. We worried that full fee-paying members would resent the £3 members, and wonder why they themselves were having to pay more than £45 and get very little extra in the way of democratic rights. We were completely opposed to holding a primary for the London Mayoral candidate, as that would cut the ground from under the feet of local Constituency Labour Parties and trade union regions.

Consultation meetings were held all over the country on the Collins proposals, and great hostility to them was expressed. The London Regional Labour Party was completely opposed to the

Mayoral primary. However, at the National Executive Committee only myself and Dennis Skinner voted against the proposals, and at the Special Conference in March 2014 the proposals were carried, as many CLPs felt they could not vote against the Leader's wishes so close to a General Election. Some other CLPs elected delegates who failed to follow their mandate. Had those of us on the Left who opposed Collins realised that the proposals would lead inexorably to Jeremy's election we would have supported them! But then, if Collins and Miliband had realised that, the proposals would certainly never have been put in the first place.

Now that we do have a pro-trade union Leader, it is to be hoped that the five year implementation timetable for cutting the affiliations down to the numbers of signed up affiliated members will be put on hold and eventually done away with altogether. There are also a great many changes to be made to the Party Rules to remedy the democratic deficit created when Blair, and later Brown, did their best to hollow out Party structures and leave members paying through the nose for very little in the way of democratic rights or the ability to hold their representatives to account.

The crowning jewel of Blair's Partnership into Power 'reforms' was the system of Policy Commissions and the National Policy Forum. At the same time, Constituency Labour Parties and trade unions were told they would no longer be able to send resolutions on topics of their choice to Annual Conference, as policy matters would now be dealt with by the Policy Forum. The only resolutions allowed would have to be 'contemporary', that is, they would have to be on a topic which had arisen since the summer meeting of the National Policy Forum. This led to all manner of tenuous 'pegs' for resolutions, that is, summer dates of speeches and announcements had to be found in order to make policy resolutions compliant with the Rules. Many such resolutions were ruled out of order by the Conference Arrangements Committee, unless they were from a right-wing Constituency Labour Party, in which case they were discovered to be contemporary, after all. The whole concept of 'contemporary' needs to be abolished so that resolutions can be put to Conference – and without having to go through a Priorities Ballot.

When the National Policy Forum was set up, we were promised

that there would be votes at the NPF and at Annual Conference, that members of Policy Commissions who disagreed with the final reports would be able to put forward minority reports, and that amendments passed at the final stage NPF would be put to Annual Conference. Almost none of this took place. The Policy Commission reports tended to be so anodyne that trying to amend them was like trying to nail blancmange to the wall. The threshold that amendments had to pass to be put to Annual Conference was set deliberately high so that, for several years, none of them made it. Large sections of the National Policy Forum made it their business to get amendments withdrawn, as voting seemed to become some kind of dirty word. The Policy Commission reports are put to Annual Conference on a take-it-or-leave-it basis. If you agree with 90 per cent of it, but disagree with 10 per cent, you either have to vote against the 90 per cent you agree with by voting against the whole report, or vote for the 10 per cent you disagree with by voting for the report.

In practice, Policy Commission reports tend to go through Conference on the nod. For several years, unions and Constituency Labour Parties have been trying to get Rule Changes through Conference to ensure that reports can be amended before being voted on. The Rule Changes have been blocked repeatedly by the Conference Arrangements Committee.

The real tragedy is that, whilst it is useful to have votes on matters of principle at Conference – for example, are we for or against Trident replacement, or are we for or against taking utilities back into public ownership – having detailed discussions of policies over time, listening to expert advice on them, and using the knowledge and expertise of rank and file members would be a very good way of making policy, and ensuring that members contributed and felt ownership at the end.

The National Policy Forum was set up promising to do all this, but then it very soon became clear that the way it was operated was intended to drive real policy discussions into the long grass – either that or bore everybody to death. The NPF needs major reform to make it work in the way that everyone originally thought it would work.

I mentioned earlier, when discussing re-selection of MPs, that local councillors had always been subject to re-selection at every local election and that no one thought anything of it. That was certainly true whilst we were having the battle over introducing mandatory re-selection for MPs, but it has not been true for some time. Over the last twenty years, Regional Labour Parties have begun interfering with councillor selections. Panels of candidates have been pruned so that there has been almost no choice for local branch members.

Candidates, including sitting councillors, have been barred from the panel of candidates so that they cannot seek election. Some areas have had the whole list of Council candidates imposed on them, not once but repeatedly during several rounds of elections. Furthermore, Blairite 'reforms' gave increasing power to the Council leader and his cabinet, so that most councillors had no influence on policy and were expected to spend all their time doing casework. Blair also encouraged arrangements for locally elected Mayors, to further decrease local accountability and concentrate power in the hands of one person who ruled through patronage and was almost impossible to unseat.

As well as allowing local members to select their Parliamentary candidates without having leadership supporters parachuted in, local councillor selections need to be freed from Regional Office interference and panels of candidates need to become lists of contact details and CVs, rather than used as a weeding out process for the politically incorrect. We need Labour to restore the democratic rights of Party members, restore and support local democracy, and take power in the town halls away from a small clique of people or an over-powerful Mayor.

If the new leadership under Jeremy Corbyn can accomplish these things, the sense of alienation that most people feel from local and national politics can be overcome. Politics needs to become what people can do together, not something which is done to them from on high.

7

Remaking the Labour Party

A Tale from the Grass Roots

Adele Williams

A personal view from an activist in the Sherwood Branch of Nottingham East Constituency Labour Party where the writer became Branch Secretary in the middle of Jeremy Corbyn's campaign for the Labour leadership.

I re-joined the Labour Party in 2009, having left in 1991. It seemed clear to me that Labour was the only viable political vehicle to get what most of us need, but I was still unsure whether it was a runner. Soon after, I was pregnant with our third child, and stunned and horrified that we'd managed to lose the election after the structural unfairness of Britain had been so brutally laid bare in the financial crisis. I could not believe that, after bailing out casino bankers, we'd not been able to offer Britain something better. We'd nationalised banks as an emergency measure, but we could not persuade either ourselves or the British people that we could do something better with the economy.

Our youngest son was walking before I made it to a branch meeting for the first time. I had been inspired to get active after seeing John McDonnell at a local meeting in 2012. I'd driven home with a little more hope about the Party, and resolved to get involved.

When I got to the branch, I found that left-leaning members were beginning to drift back into the Party, and that some had stood steadfast and never left. Around the same time, I became active with the People's Assembly in Nottingham. We launched campaigns on austerity's impact on food poverty, against the privatisation of the NHS and our wider public services and, as the election grew nearer, we launched, with the support of Unite, the *Nottingham We Deserve* anti-austerity newspaper. We posted this through doors in the city, and the marginal constituencies at the borders of Nottingham in an effort to bring our anti-austerity message home. A well-organised and agile campaign, Nottingham People's Assembly drew large numbers to its events, giving a voice and organisation to the anti-austerity mood in the city.

As the election approached, many anti-austerity activists moved into the Party and worked for Labour victories in the marginal seats surrounding the city. On election night, we were devastated to discover that, though we had increased our share of the vote in the Nottingham city constituencies, we'd lost in the surrounding target seats such as Broxtowe and Sherwood. We'd allowed the Tories to define the narrative on the economy, and the doorstep chorus of 'they're all the same' should have given us advance warning that the polls were wrong.

Right after the general election and before Jeremy's leadership bid, even more people began to join the Party across Nottingham. People had expected a Labour victory, and when it didn't happen they were galvanised to act.

As the leadership election commenced, we were dismayed that a sizeable stream of opinion in the Party was to be unrepresented in the range of candidates. I was at a Peoples' Assembly and Unite Community meeting on the night that Jeremy announced that he'd stand. I was initially sceptical that he'd be able to get the nominations he needed from fellow MPs but, like many others, I joined the campaign, largely on social media, to build pressure to open the gates of Party democracy. This social media campaign was coordinated and facilitated by *Red Labour* but, like much of the campaign, also sprang from new and re-inspired activists who felt compelled to act.

It was when Jeremy got over the threshold of 35 nominations from Labour MPs, on 15 June, that new members began to really flood in. In the three months between Jeremy getting the nominations and the day before the results were announced, we'd increased the size of our branch by 36 per cent. The percentage increase from the date of Parliamentary nominations and the end of October was 90 per cent. Overall, since the general election, our membership has increased by 122 per cent. Ours is now the largest Labour Party branch in the East Midlands, but this growth trend appears to be typical.

Nottingham held two rallies as part of Jeremy's campaign: one early on in the campaign and one towards the end of it. Sunday lunchtime is not the prime slot for a political meeting, but the

Bertrand Russell Peace Foundation rally with Corbyn packed City Arts' exhibition space with activists looking for both hope and an opportunity to contribute. Jeremy later told the BBC that he'd first thought that something was happening after speaking to that packed hall on a Sunday lunchtime in Nottingham. Later into the campaign, people queued round the block to hear Jeremy at the historic Albert Hall and hundreds waited patiently to hear him speak outside.

Nottingham activists, like many around the country, also ran street stalls, recruiting to Labour and meeting a surprising number of new and existing members keen to support Corbyn. The Corbyn campaign's phone banks drew in members and non-members, young new activists and re-inspired ex-members from all walks of life. Conversations with existing members were encouraging, and gave the lie to the charge of entryism. I loved the phone banking. Calling the Labour members from Unite's Nottingham office, it became clear that Jeremy's campaign was inspiring people who'd had a bellyful of triangulated policy and wanted to hear Labour offering a clear and principled narrative that would ring true with the electorate.

It was clear to me by this point that that we'd win, but our huge victory in all sections of the Party was magnificent, and a reflection of the hope and energy that Jeremy's campaign had generated.

There is no one in the Party churlish enough to suggest that Jeremy's ability to inspire hope and action is not in large part responsible for the steep increase in membership and activism. It's worth taking a minute to think about what that means for our clout as a Party. Instead of the four million conversations we were able to have at the last election, we can confidently plan to have 8 million, and with a Party of one million, which is surely within our grasp, we can be talking to a significant proportion of the electorate in person – and with a clear and credible message. The real impact is bigger, of course, for our new members are enthusiastic, on average a little younger, and have, in the main, come to the Party both willing and expecting to become activists.

We have learnt that we cannot fight the Tories with Tory policies, and we know we cannot compete with their grip on the mainstream media, or their coffers. Our breadth and depth in communities all over Britain will be the basis from which we can hope to win in 2020 and every possible election in between. The extent to which we are knitted into every community will be key to this, and to making the Party's active membership function as ballast for Jeremy's leadership.

After Jeremy's election, our branch meetings immediately changed character. Doubling in size, and filled with new members, they presented us with a challenge to engage these new activists, to maintain and build on their enthusiasm. Large meetings can be unwieldy and it's difficult to contribute meaningfully, so we have tried to encourage small action groups to work on specific projects that they will shape and bring to the branch to ask for support and resources.

We've all talked a lot about the potential for a grassroots, organised mass movement to circumvent the broadcast and print media. To do that, we need to normalise and humanise political discussion and campaigning. I first had the feeling that things were really changing when I talked on the bus to a young woman with an NHS badge about joining as a supporter to back Jeremy. It wasn't that she did join that made me think that things were different; it was the lack of awkwardness in that previously unlikely situation. If we're going to normalise 'talking politics' on the bus, at work, in the shop, we have to model it in the way we conduct ourselves in branch meetings. This process is helped by the fact that we're now seeing the people we know from the bus, at work, in the shop *at* branch meetings. So some members will have to learn to curtail long-winded 'expositions' of political theory and make sure that new and possibly less confident members get a voice. We need to remodel branch meetings to bring in those quieter members, whilst retaining our democratic apparatus.

It's often said that our new members have little appetite or patience for minutes, matters arising, and the 'business' of meetings. There is some squeamishness about the formalities of meetings, and they should definitely be kept in their place, but we also have to remember that the democratic structures of the Party have been degraded and will need to be rebuilt. Our minutes and motions will underpin that process, so let's not be too shamefaced about them. If the minutes tell a story of a growing movement that is challenging for power through community-based campaigning, I don't think our new members will judge us too harshly.

New members of the Party have not arrived with the intention of passively backing Jeremy. They want to engage with the Party's policy making and they are certainly not all of the same shade of red. Jeremy's pledges on open Party democracy were very powerful in the campaign. We need to make the bones of our democracy more visible to allow these members to engage with policy making. Policy should begin in branch meetings, go through the CLP, get to conference, and end up in Parliament, but at the moment, those routes are unclear and contentious. We need to make the gap between democratic decision making at branch level and national party policy more visible as a start towards closing it, in order to build a robust policy making structure. No one should be elected to anything in our Party without a statement of their views and approach, and we need to work to establish that as a principle – and to encourage people of all shades of opinion to stand for Party positions and positions of office with the expectation that an open and respectful debate will take place. I don't believe that even one of our new members has joined to seek office of any kind, but I'll be doing my best to suggest that they consider it. Becoming a mass membership organisation with a significant activist base will change the terrain of selections completely, and opens up the real possibility of a Parliamentary Party that not only reflects the Party itself but reflects our nation.

To engage these new members and more, all branch mailings should be activist bulletins, both in terms of party campaigns and those of trade unions and other community groups. We are working hard to strengthen the connections across the Labour Movement, building concrete solidarity, and also ensuring that trade unions are well represented at CLP level. We share information on community campaigns, trade union activity and Labour campaigning through our email lists and social media.

It certainly isn't clear yet, though, how best to organise our new members. Many have suggested that we should organise at a micro level in our communities, and that social action could be one way to strengthen our roots and engage both our new members and those yet to join.

When canvassing on election day, I met a very old man. We chatted through his window as he was too unwell to come to the door. He talked about his days in the youth wing of the party, and of how young members used to help out the older people. As our public services are stripped back down to the barest minimum and less, is it time for us to re-engage with Labour's heritage of local action that embeds our roots in the community, giving us the connections and credibility to raise the big issues? Owen Jones has raised the social action undertaken by Syriza as a model to engage Labour's new army of activists, and to embed the party in the broader community. However, such action will need to be approached in innovative ways to involve those new members with busy lives. Like many Labour branches, we collect for a local foodbank, but we don't yet run one, though individual members may be involved.

Our new members, like many of our longstanding members, are subject to the same pressures on their time as the rest of the population. It is possibly more acute amongst our newer members though, as Jeremy's victory has inspired people to commit to the Party who wouldn't otherwise have thought they had the spare time to commit to anything. Our members have caring responsibilities and jobs that are unpredictable, or spill over into their evenings and weekends.

There's a crisis in volunteering in general due to demographic changes and work creeping into home life. The third sector has responded by offering 'micro-volunteering' opportunities. We should seek to offer flexible ways for people to contribute their time and ideas, whether online or in person. In our branch we're planning daytime events so that people with children who struggle to get out in the evenings for meetings can be involved and be encouraged to become active. We're trying to offer new people the opportunity to self-organise on campaigns, whilst the branch retains oversight of the 'message' and resources. Branch meetings are often a gateway to campaigning, so if members aren't able to attend those, we need to build other routes into activism.

I discovered recently that one of our local branches still has 'block stewards' who post mail locally and let their near neighbours know about meetings and campaigning. We have built analogues of this process online, but we need to reintroduce this on our streets as a framework for local organising. I recognise that this is an easier proposition in Nottingham East than it might be in less traditionally Labour or urban areas. We could, though, have been organised like that in our ward even before our massive membership growth. Outside elections, though, Labour Party politics was not so visible in the community, other than in the positive impacts of a Labour council. Many of us who were active in the Poll Tax campaign will remember how locally it was organised. A very local presence will connect the Party to the community and its issues, and normalise the idea that a political campaigning response is both viable and essential if we are to defend our communities from the worst of what the Tories have planned.

We must continue to build and extend online, but we must also reconnect the social and community bonds that once underpinned the Labour movement. Labour branches are making these changes, and developing community action projects as I write.

With our growing membership, we can put into practice the lessons we can learn from Unite Community's organising model, identifying issues and using them as a focus for mobilising collective action. We need to be there, working alongside Unite Community or the People's Assembly. Labour should be making the connections between campaigns, and the broader issues we want our people in Parliament to fight for. When we are involved, and our representatives are involved in community campaigns, it's not enough to say what Labour would have done if we were in power. We need to tell them what we will do right now.

We now have a Labour Party leadership that really understands campaigning and the importance of building and mobilising from the grassroots. We have thousands of new members full of hope and energy. We actually can make Labour awesome again.

8
The 'Unelectable' Elected Man
Abi Rhodes

With minutes to go before Big Ben struck noon on the 15 June 2015, the 100/1 outsider Jeremy Corbyn squeezed his name onto the Labour leadership ballot paper. Reaching the 35 MP threshold for the initial nomination process turned out to be one of the many difficult obstacles for 'Team Jeremy' to climb. His stated reason for standing for the leadership came from a desire to ensure that a full and rounded debate about the future of the Labour Party would be had. And open up the debate he did. Over the next few months, as the leadership contest heated up, political heavyweights such as Tony Blair, Gordon Brown and Peter Mandelson entered the fray, supported by the likes of Jon Cruddas and (Lord) John Hutton, who were following up their post-mortems of the lifeless body of the Labour Party post-2015 election.

After the monumental disappointment of the general election, the rhetoric that 'Labour was too left wing to win' advocated the view that there was no appetite amongst the electorate for a socialist or egalitarian construction of society. Yet the groundswell of support for the anti-austerity message of social movements such as *The People's Assembly Against Austerity*, plus substantial support for Jeremy Corbyn during his leadership election campaign, pointed in the opposite direction, suggesting that Labour was not left wing enough. The British national press, aided by a number of senior Labour Party members, claimed that a left-wing Labour platform would be unelectable. New Labour's critique of the Party under Miliband was simply consistent with the dominant neoliberal narrative that left-leaning, or socialist, politics is a danger to the public good. This view conveniently ignores the empirical evidence that the English electorate are hungry for just such an alternative to the present societal arrangement.

Shortly after the election defeat in May 2015, Lord Hutton, in a *Newsnight* interview, and Jon Cruddas, in an independent review, proffered the view that anti-austerity was not what the public needed. Hutton claimed that:

There's a limited appetite, a dwindling appetite for the old-school socialist menu which we had on offer. I think we've really got to be grown up now and take a long, hard look at ourselves and ask ourselves the question what sort of party we want to be.[1]

There are several assumptions underlying this statement that, once teased out, can be used to challenge Hutton's view of society. Chief amongst these is the view that the Labour Party exists as an entity that must decide on its own stance and direction, independent of the individual views of its members. Secondly, Lord Hutton's statement seems to assume that any appetite for 'old-school' socialism that may exist is now confined to history, and that such an idealistic, immature position must be abandoned if the Labour Party is to 'grow up' and become a political force again. Finally, there is the all-important value assumption that, after a 'long, hard look at ourselves', Labour's immature offering of socialism should be discarded in favour of something more mature. This is reminiscent of the reprimand a disappointed parent might give a naughty teenager. Such assumptions necessarily imply that the alternative neoliberal, capitalist structuring of society is the desired and 'mature' view, and one that Hutton has clearly decided is the favoured approach of the electorate in Britain.

A few months later, Jon Cruddas reiterated Lord Hutton's political line in his Independent Inquiry into why Labour lost the election, the conclusion of which was:

... that the Tories didn't win despite austerity, they won because of it. Voters did not reject Labour because they saw it as austerity lite. Voters rejected Labour because they perceived the Party as anti-austerity lite.[2]

The report found that 58 per cent of the 3,000 people surveyed agreed that cutting the deficit was a top priority during the election and deduces that, 'the unpalatable truth for the left is that the Tories did not win despite austerity, but because of it'. Perhaps, if a survey had been conducted of the tens of thousands of people, whether or not they were Labour voters in May, who attended Jeremy Corbyn's hustings up and down the country during his campaign, then the inquiry might have produced wildly different results. It may have put forth the argument that voters rejected Labour because it wasn't anti-austerity enough. Instead, Cruddas gathered data and chose to analyse it in a particular way, one that remains confined within the mould set by the assumption that the centre ground is where political debates are won and lost. Corbyn, from the outset, was determined to break that mould and have a different kind of debate.

But the cast was (and still is) a hard one to smash. Tony Blair was not so subtle in his prognosis of Labour's future or the desires of the electorate. In an assault on Jeremy Corbyn that appeared mid-campaign, the former leader's pleas to the electorate were apocalyptic in tone. In an article published in *The Guardian* in August, he hysterically claimed that if Jeremy Corbyn became Labour leader the Party wouldn't just face defeat, but total annihilation. His opening sentence, 'The Labour Party is in danger more mortal today than at any point in the over 100 years of its existence', echoes the assumptions inherent in Lord Hutton's verdict, that the Labour Party is an entity that can be fatally wounded. The value assumption behind Blair's statement lies baldly in the neoliberal camp that a Corbyn (and thus a socialist) win would make the Labour Party unelectable. In a speech in London entitled *Power for a Purpose*, Gordon Brown reiterated the mantra that the Labour Party needs to be 'electable ... popular, and not simply a party of protest ...' in order to be returned to government in 2020. While his speech was a thinly veiled attack on Corbyn, Peter Mandelson went all out by appealing to the three mainstream candidates to quit the leadership contest *en masse*, in the hope that it would be suspended.

All these reactions reflect the (neoliberal) assumption that being left wing is somehow so utterly unpalatable that the electorate should find the thought of it thoroughly stomach turning. It fundamentally misunderstands the nature of an idea such as socialism, forgetting who and what the Labour Party was set up to represent, as well as ignoring the nature of the electorate as a dynamic, free-thinking force.

That there exists an entity that is the Labour Party is indisputable, but it is an organic body composed of *all* its members. The same is true for the electorate. The notion that these collectives could be torn asunder by an idea such as socialism is so transparently untrue as to be laughable. Especially if the concept is described in the manner of the late Tony Benn, who elucidated its real meaning when he enunciated the idea as '*Social*-ism', and explained that it is about trying to construct a society around production for need and not just for profit. Cruddas in his review acknowledges that the majority of the electorate understand that the economic system, as it is presently constructed, is inherently unfair. And it is this injustice that Corbyn is seeking to challenge with his reinvigorated debate about the meaning of socialism and the future of the Labour Party.

So how has Jeremy Corbyn managed to ignite such passionate discussion among hundreds of thousands of people across the UK? One answer is that he offers a real alternative to the homogeneity of the established political class, many of whom consider politics to be nothing more than a career move. It is becoming increasingly self-evident that a large proportion of the electorate is beginning to think that another way is indeed possible. Even before the leadership campaign truly got underway, this view was borne out by the success of *The People's Assembly Against Austerity's* demonstration of 20 June 2015. An enormous cheer went up for Jeremy as he addressed those assembled in Parliament Square. He asked those present to 'stand up as the brave people did in the 1920s and 1930s' to ask for 'a state that takes responsibility for everybody – to ensure that nobody is destitute ... everybody caring for everybody else. I think it is called socialism'. It was clear from the crowd's response that the appetite for a more egalitarian way of organising society is burgeoning. Commentators who suggest that socialism is dead, or that a vote for Jeremy is to render the Labour Party unelectable, clearly haven't met the electorate! There were 250,000 of them stood in front of Westminster one weekend in June, all calling for an alternative to austerity and celebrating the prospect of that being socialism.

Further evidence of the hunger for an alternative to the homogeneity offered up by the centre ground is the fact that Jeremy Corbyn received the largest mandate of any Labour leader in the history of the Party. Corbyn received 59.5% of first-preference votes, having gained the support of 49.6% of full members and 57.6% of affiliated (mainly Trade Union) supporters, and he managed to do this in the face of rampant establishment hostility. By sidestepping the mainstream media, an (almost) unmediated political message could be disseminated. Away from, and in spite of, the influence of voices such as Blair, Brown and Mandelson's, Team Corbyn, and the man himself, presented to the electorate 'straight talking, honest politics'.

The effectiveness of Jeremy Corbyn's leadership campaign was the ability to quickly assemble hustings up and down the country, largely via a strong network of tens of thousands of volunteers in sync with social media. As the contribution by Ben Sellers in this book lays bare, the reach of such an anonymous social media collective is extensive. During the three months of the leadership election, the 'Jeremy Corbyn for Leader' Facebook page and the 'JeremyCorbyn4Leader' Twitter profile attracted tens of thousands of likes and followers respectively. These spawned many regional offshoots. Meetings were organised in the blink of an eye as the #JezWeCan meme took off. The positive, organic enthusiasm of Corbyn's grassroots supporters translated into the historic election result for the new Labour leader.

To date, since becoming Leader, Jeremy Corbyn is weathering the mainstream media storm, which vehemently and constantly upholds the view that the UK does not want socialism and that there is no alternative. This is largely due to bypassing of the dominant narrative by social media and social movement campaigns, but it is also thanks to the huge appetite people have for the ideas put forth by Jeremy. The value assumptions inherent in the statements analysed earlier are being challenged by the new politics and Corbyn is changing the fundamental consistency of Labour, by including *all* members of the party. Politics in the Marxist sense, as that concerning social relations, given half a chance might actually transform the political arena from the Punch and Judy Show that is Party Politics into something that, without any other agenda, is focused on ensuring a fair and equal slice of the cake for all.

With the renewed vigour of the Labour Party under Jeremy Corbyn's leadership, and his desire to develop a new kind of politics in association with grassroots movements, more people are now re-engaging with the political system. If the momentum continues it is possible that a Labour government will be elected in 2020 on a socialist platform and that many more commentators than Paddy Ashdown will be eating their hats!

Notes

1. *https://www.youtube.com/watch?v=G04yBNTnmug&list=PLJxnQXiytA_Tt3SR_GROIO2dzFXhXHggr*
2. *http://labourlist.org/2015/08/labour-lost-because-voters-believed-it-was-anti austerity/*

PART 3

Changing our World?

9
The Motive Force of Empire
Jeremy Corbyn MP

In 2011, Jeremy Corbyn contributed this Foreword to Spokesman's new edition of J A Hobson's influential classic, Imperialism: A Study, *first published in 1902.*

J. A. Hobson wrote his great tome at a different age. His thoughts were dominated by the zenith of the British Empire and the Boer War. The outcome of the war demonstrated Britain's then ability in sustaining global reach, since Elizabethan times, but also its extreme vulnerability. At home the poor physique of working class soldiers led to Haldane's investigation into working class health and living conditions. The difficulty in containing the rebellious Boers, and the huge opposition to the war, encouraged further doubts about the whole Empire project.

What was remarkable was that Hobson wrote Imperialism at the end of the scramble for Africa in which Britain had gained enormous tracts of land, and Rhodes was busying himself with the Cape to Cairo railway project. The most cynical of western manoeuvres, the Congress of Berlin in 1884, had agreed on the lines on the map, which largely still exist and have been the cause of endless wars and the loss of many lives.

What is interesting is the way in which Hobson contrasts the 'new' African Empire and global reach that Britain had finally gained for itself with the two earlier editions of Britain's empire. The American Empire had collapsed in the eighteenth century, when the thirteen colonies rebelled and finally gained their independence; British efforts to re-take them were unsuccessful. Even despite the US Civil War, the new power over the water was now almost as great as the old imperial powers of France, Britain and Spain.

In effect, Hobson accepts that America had gone, and that the analysis should be looking at the dilemma between the 'real' British Empire in India and the new one in Africa and scattered islands across the oceans.

For someone who was revered by Marxists, and quoted by Lenin, for his analysis of the pressures to extend empire, his analysis of the then current empire, and its future, was not very revolutionary. What is brilliant, and very controversial at the time, is his analysis of the pressures that were hard at work in pushing for a vast national effort in grabbing new outposts of Empire on distant islands and shores. His painstaking analysis of the costs, and the alleged benefits, of Empire is very powerful.

Pages of trade statistics show how the vast military spending on naval escorts, army postings and the human costs of wars had made little difference to Britain's trade in comparison to those countries who had little or no overseas places but successfully traded. The characterisation of the political and commercial interests that fed the cause of new empire is almost a parallel for our times. Then, as now, the popular press presented a general view of British superiority over the rest of the world, which effectively opened a space for the unholy alliance of an ambitious military high command and huge commercial interests. This created opportunities for arms manufacturers, business for shipping companies, and protected closed markets for British companies. It was also the mainstay of what had become traditional British industries such as cotton. Thousands of people were working in mills all across Lancashire and Yorkshire making products from raw materials which were imported over thousands of miles, and exported in reverse over the same routes.

What is attractive is Hobson's ability to separate and disassemble the interests of the commercial and imperial aims. He makes the valid point that other European countries, without the benefit of empires, manage to be successful trading and industrial powers in their own right.

Hobson's railing against the commercial interests that fuel the role of the popular press with tales of imperial might, that then lead on to racist caricatures of African and Asian peoples, was both correct and prescient. The way in which the British press portrayed Ghandi in the 1930s, or Kenyatta in the 1950s or, indeed, Argentina's soldiers and sailors in the 1980s shows the tricks have not changed dramatically.

The other relationship that has not changed at all is the link of these interests to the supposed national interest and the parroting of prejudices in Parliament. From John Bull and Cecil Rhodes in the nineteenth century, the khaki politicians who encouraged thousands to their deaths in 1914, and then the later colonial and imperial wars, the cynical manipulation has continued. Indeed, as with previous wars, there were deliberate media and political attempts to denigrate whole peoples in the run up to the wars in Iraq and Afghanistan.

Hobson's comments in Chapter V when he says that 'the increased hostility of foreign nations towards us in the last thirty years of the nineteenth century may be regarded as entirely due to the aggressive imperialism of those years …' are a clear assertion of the real process that was taking place. This is followed by a table of costs that demonstrates how colonial trade rose from £184 millions in 1884 to £232 millions in 1903, but that arms costs went from £27 millions to £123 millions in 1902. This vast expenditure, a four-fold rise in eighteen years, (partly occasioned by the Boer War) encouraged the intensity of the growing arms race and colonial competition between Britain and Germany.

Hobson describes the way that the conglomeration of Army and Naval Officers, serving and retired, media opinion formers and the whole retinue of manufacturers and arms dealers created a juggernaut that cost the nation, and ultimately, the world, dear.

In Chapter VII of his book Hobson develops a thesis that, to me, is strange, and at variance with the general analysis he presents against empire. He discusses the issues of organisation and activity of an empire and seems to be heading, in part, in the direction of some kind of Anglo Saxon Empire. This was long before the French idea of Overseas Departments and a global empire based on the cultural norms of the mother country. In this section Hobson makes some very prescient comments on the cultural identity and power of both India and China. Now emerging as the two most populous nations in the world and of ever increasing importance. In 1902, neither was united as a nation, both were wholly or partly occupied and controlled by European powers. His analysis was based on the obvious issues of population and resources, but also on the understanding of the colonial and technical traditions of both countries. China was clearly the most pre-eminent power for most of the past millennium and is now, in reality, returning to the technical pre-eminence it enjoyed before the European industrial revolutions.

What Hobson also observed was the growing industrial and imperial power of China; expansion and casting an eye towards the Pacific. In very prescient observations he saw military rivalry with the United States. Forty years later, a vicious conflict was in full swing between the USA and Japan in World War Two.

Reading Hobson's works now, at the end of the first decade of the twenty first century, and acknowledging all that has happened in the huge sweep of imperial and post colonial history, he deserves enormous credit and recognition. At his time of writing the British Empire was at its zenith, as were the French and German empires. The European powers were feeling very pleased with themselves, having divided Africa amongst themselves at the Congress of Berlin in 1884. They also accepted the Monroe Doctrine, which gave the United States the whip hand over the former Spanish colonies of Latin America. US power, already huge, and its armed forces, soon to become more than a match for the Europeans, were honed from their domestic arms race in the civil war. Active in aggression and occupation in Mexico, Cuba, the Philippines, their forces were ideally equipped for their initially reluctant participation in the Great War.

The Europeans, meanwhile, were concerning themselves with the challenge of the declining Ottoman Empire. National competition, huge leaps in arms technology, and nationalist rhetoric encouraged the descent into the abyss of the First World War. The millions who died in the trenches and mud of the Western Front laid down their lives for each other's empires. The whole allied edifice came crashing down when Russia withdrew, following the revolution, the Germans surrendered, and faced the arrogance of the victorious allies in Versailles.

The complexities of Versailles are often presented as the end of Empire but were, in fact, a change of gear and approach whilst preserving the colonial sensitivities of Britain and France. The German colonies were divided up between the victorious powers, while the Ottoman Empire was divided into the now notorious 'mandates'. Woodrow Wilson and his 'fourteen points' were the high point of articulation of then American liberal thinking, but tinged with more than a nod towards rapidly developing industrial and military US power.

Even as the great powers were humiliating Germany at Versailles and sharing out the spoils of war, they were united in detestation of the nascent Soviet Union. An alliance of all the victorious powers was equipping the Tsarist forces and fighting the Red Army. The Soviet Union survived, and expelled those forces as huge workers' risings were taking place in Europe, particularly Germany.

The era of traditional empire was over, but was Imperial thinking? Britain and France clung on to their colonial possessions with increasing difficulty and inability to pay for the rising military cost of subjecting people in revolt against the notion of distant European control of their lives. Both countries indulged in grand self delusions of huge buildings such as Lutyens' palaces in New Delhi and attempts at uniting the empire with new shipping and airlines. Astonishingly, at a time of depression and rapid economic decline at home, Imperial Airways was presented as a step forward; there were massive Empire Day festivities and grand Royal tours of the Empire.

The costs of World War Two and the loss of prestige of the European colonialists did not prevent Britain, France and The Netherlands attempting to re-take their 'possessions' in Asia from the Japanese and return to the 1930s. In the case of Vietnam and Indonesia, this was done with the enlisted support of surrendered and then conscripted Japanese soldiers.

Suspicion of Britain and France's role in their colonies temporarily fuelled American suspicions of a war to re-create empires. Britain was forced into independence of the Indian Subcontinent in 1947 and the catastrophic partition into India and Pakistan. France lost the battle of Dien Bien Phu in 1954, and was thus forced out of Indochina. Colonial wars followed but, by the end of the 1960s, European empires in the sense of colonial possessions were over.

Empires collapse from a combination of factors, principally the difficulty of governing and sustaining a regime at a distance, but also from opposition to the whole notion of empire at home. The two pre-eminent European colonial powers of the twentieth century, Britain and France, both had enormous confusions on the left about empire. Both countries had been through political revolution, which was immediately followed by racial and political acts of contradiction to the supposed ethics of the new forces. Cromwell, having defeated the monarchist forces in the Civil War in 1648, invaded and occupied Ireland in unparalleled brutality and savagery. The uprising of black slaves in Haiti, in 1798, was brutally repressed by French forces sent by Napoleon in the name of Liberty, Equality and Fraternity.

In a sense, that confusion and contradiction remained with the British left who supported Empire Free Trade and dominion status in the 1920s. Elements of the French left initially supported the war against independence for Algeria in the 1950s.

In many ways the military disaster of the Suez adventure in 1956, when Britain and France tried to prevent Egypt from nationalising the Suez Canal, was the end of their empires. The United States and the Soviet Union became the big poles in the globe and in their own ways developed empires of ideology and economy.

Since World War Two, the big imperial force has been the United States on behalf of global capitalism and the biggest, mostly US-based corporations. The propaganda for this has presented itself as a voice for 'freedom' and carefully and consciously conflated it with market economics.

The 1949 Congress for Cultural Freedom in Amsterdam was the European opening to accompany the military re-occupation under the guise of NATO. Thus, the Cold War was followed by American media and cultural values, in an attempt to create an empire of the mind. The hard power of their weaponry, the malign influence of the CIA, and its creation of pliant and friendly governments actively suppressed and subjugated peoples in the poorest counties of the world.

The influence of the Soviet Union around the world was huge, but tempered by an inadequate industrial base in comparison to the United States and the ruinously expensive arms race that hastened its decline, and eventual collapse in 1990. But the Soviet influence was always different, and its allies often acted quite independently. Cuba, desperately dependent on Soviet support for its survival in the 1960s through to the 1980s, developed a quite independent foreign policy and enormous respect and stature amongst the poorest people, particularly in Latin America.

What the Cubans and, in particular, Che Guevara were preaching in the 1960s has an even greater resonance today in the left of Latin America. The popular socialist movements of Bolivia, Ecuador and Venezuela owe much to his vision. The Bolivarian alliance, with its economic and social justice requirements, represents a challenge and appeal that the traditional Monroe Doctrine of military power accompanied by global capital cannot match at all.

If the US has problems in Latin America, it has far greater problems in relation to Islam and its behaviour around the world. Like all empires, the excessive use of natural resources and huge costs of its military create the paradigms of decline and collapse. The US has, since the end of World War Two, sought access to markets and materials. Challenged by OPEC in the 1970s, it has desperately tried to control and hang on to influence in the Middle East. Some of this thinking led to the wars in Iraq in 1990 and 2003.

Bush and Blair's assertion of the War on Terror in 2001 had as much to do with economic interests as any notion of 'security'. Afghanistan, the longest lasting US military involvement apart from Vietnam, is fuelled by notions of security and assertion of military power, but also of the huge unexploited mineral reserves. The irony of Afghanistan is that the unsuccessful attempts by the western counties to occupy and control will probably lead to Chinese mineral extraction to fuel their industries. It would bring a wry smile to Hobson, who long predicted the rise of China at the expense of the western powers.

The huge issues facing the world are of unprecedented shortages of raw materials, food and land coupled with enormous military expenditure and a huge gulf between the richest and poorest. A sixth of the world's population are permanently hungry, the same number again are politely described as 'food insecure', whilst the ominous issues of overdevelopment, water shortages and loss of ecology, and thus sustainability, mount up.

Free market capitalism cannot provide for everyone, or sustain the natural world. Its very imperative is of ever hastening exploitation of all resources including people, and it needs armies and weapons to secure those supplies. The political appeal, unchallenged in the 1990s, of this concept is fast fading by a combination of Islamic opposition and the radical popular movements of landless and poor peoples in many poor countries. Increasingly, these movements also have a resonance in the cities of the industrial countries as well.

All empires asserted themselves by technology. The Greek and Persian Empires by language and communications, the Romans by settlement, efficient armies and technology of agriculture and craft. The huge empires of China were technologically well in advance of any other for several centuries. Despite not having the use of the wheel, horses or steam power, the American empires of Aztec, Inca and Maya could dominate and control through advanced technology of building and communications, and, of course, disciplined forces.

The brutality of European expansion from the sixteenth century was based on superior weaponry and industry, and the waging of a permanent cultural war both at home and in the occupied lands. The racist stereotyping of peoples by the Europeans allowed the slave trade to develop and prosper. It enabled the most appalling degradation of subjected peoples to take place and pour untold wealth into pockets of the merchant classes in the cities of Britain and Europe.

Culture is an important part of empire, as is source of knowledge and understanding of history. All countries encourage a very nationalist form of history teaching, and from that stems racism and perverted feelings of superiority.

Technology cannot be monopolised any longer nor communication really be brought under control. The whole world has realised the lack of emperors' clothes through Wikileaks; the honesty of the imperial masters in the global market place is now forever under scrutiny.

However, the wars and conflict are about poverty and hunger and the competition of the powerful for resources. Thus, big corporations, with the support of national governments, grab land in the poorest counties to supply food and fuel for the future. Desperately poor people in Kenya and Guatemala watch as land is fenced in and luscious genetically modified crops are produced and flown out to feed the well-fed on overnight flights.

Migrant flows of people in desperate search of work and life occur all over the world; at any one time there are probably 200 million people on the move in search of a sustainable life. These people, the most exploited, are the Fourth World who travel and hope and try and survive, but often die on roads and railway lines, in seas and in poverty.

Western countries in Europe and the United States are finding they do not really control their own economies, that the contradictions of global capital are bigger than they are. They also realise that none of the world's institutions can really control anything. The United Nations, long seen as a hope for peace and order, has such limited power and resources it can only proclaim, not control any situation.

The wars that are now being fought are of ideas and economic power. The free market model cannot sustain or succeed; the more collectivist approach of the Non-Aligned Movement, and assertion of the needs of the poorer countries of the world, does provide hope.

However, the denial of individual and collective rights, opportunities for women, and the increasing polarisation between rich and poor contain the seeds of conflicts to come. The writings of Arundhati Roy, as a voice for the voiceless and oppressed, are as prescient for the future as any.

Hobson proclaimed against the absurdity and inadequacy of empire. In this era we need sustainability and justice. Neither is possible in an ideology committed to aggrandizement of wealth. A century ago, Hobson analysed the motive force of Empire in an era of uniforms, deference and unnecessary respect for power and authority. That ideology has been replaced by an obsession with money and exploitation, and it is just as pernicious and equally dangerous for the future.

10

Internationalist at Work

Some Impressions

Tony Simpson

Jeremy Corbyn (Islington North) (Lab): I echo the Prime Minister's tributes to the two RAF airmen killed in Afghanistan, Flight Lieutenant Geraint Roberts and Flight Lieutenant Alan Scott, and also the sadness at the death of David Phillips in the line of duty, as many police officers do face danger. I absolutely concur with the Prime Minister's remarks about that. I am sure the Prime Minister and the whole House would also join me in expressing sympathies and sadness at the more than 100 people who died in a bomb blast in Ankara last Sunday, attending a peace rally of all things, and our sympathies must go to all of them.

Now Leader of the Labour Party, and of Her Majesty's Loyal Opposition in Parliament, Jeremy Corbyn asks questions of the British Prime Minister on a weekly basis. On 14 October 2015, he joined David Cameron in offering condolences to the families of two RAF airmen recently killed in distant Afghanistan and of a policeman deliberately run over whilst on duty in Wallasey on Merseyside.

Mr Corbyn also reminded the assembled Members of Parliament of the terrible bombings in Ankara the previous weekend, which had killed more than 100 people who were calling for peace in the run-up to the November 2015 general election in Turkey. Most of those killed were Kurds, who form a substantial minority in Turkey. For the second time in a few months, their party, the People's Democratic Party (HDP), was to pass the excessively high ten per cent threshold to enter the Turkish Parliament. The large Kurdish community in Turkey struggles to maintain its due parliamentary representation in the face of long-term oppression and persecution by the Turkish State and the Justice and Development Party (AK) of President Erdogan.

Turkey has a huge military, is a prominent and active member of the North Atlantic Treaty Organisation (NATO), and houses US nuclear gravity bombs on its territory. Currently, millions of refugees from the war in Syria face another bleak winter in Turkey, although hundreds of thousands continue to travel north in the hope of reaching Germany and some other countries of the European Union which will admit them. The journey is perilous, tiring and expensive; an index of their desperation. On winning election to the leadership of the Labour Party, Jeremy Corbyn's first public engagement was to address a rally welcoming and supporting refugees, recognising the constructive contributions they make to the communities in which they settle.

Jeremy Corbyn brings a breath of fresh, international air to the top of British Parliamentary politics. But his range and reach are much wider than Westminster. For years, he has engaged with long-running campaigns such as Kurdish aspirations for effective political representation and the release of their imprisoned leader, Abdullah Ocalan, whom the Turks wanted to execute after abducting him in Nairobi, en route to meet Nelson Mandela, in 1999. Since then, Ocalan, who founded the Kurdistan Workers' Party (PKK), has been held in solitary confinement on the island of Imrali in the Sea of Marmara, close to Istanbul. From there, he continues to exert considerable influence on the millions of oppressed Kurds, repeatedly advocating a peaceful solution to the long-term armed conflict between Kurds and Turks in Turkey and over the border, in Iraq. Jeremy Corbyn's condolences for the victims of the Ankara bombs will have been heard in Diyarbakir, the unofficial Kurdish capital in south-eastern Turkey, as well as in Ankara and Istanbul.

The Kurdish issue may be taken as one among many examples of Corbyn's internationalism, which is grounded in a clear recognition of the need for justice and environmental sustainability, as well as a genuine curiosity about what is happening in different corners of the world. His support for the demands of Turkey's oppressed Kurds sits alongside his outspoken advocacy of the long-standing claims of the Palestinian people in Israel, Palestine and the diaspora; another instance of Corbyn's long-term and active commitment. As occupying Israelis shoot on sight in Bethlehem and Hebron, young Palestinian men and women bleed to death before our eyes. Years ago, Corbyn travelled the open rolling hills of Palestine, and has seen that landscape carved up and walled with the passage of decades.

Corbyn's engagement and active solidarity with oppressed peoples in different continents endures, as does his strong sense of history, which is much in evidence in his commentary on J. A. Hobson's influential book, *Imperialism: A Study*, reprinted elsewhere in this collection. Corbyn concludes his survey of Hobson's Study with these words:

> *Hobson proclaimed against the absurdity and inadequacy of empire. In this era we need sustainability and justice. Neither is possible in an ideology committed to aggrandisement of wealth. A century ago, Hobson analysed the motive force of Empire in an era of uniforms, deference and unnecessary respect for power and authority. That ideology has been replaced by an obsession with money and exploitation, and it is just as pernicious and equally dangerous for the future.*

Corbyn brings personal warmth, humility and humanity in confronting such dangers. In late autumn 2015, Shaker Aamer returned to his family in Britain from Guantanamo Bay, after being held for 14 years without charge. His is one of the more egregious instances of the all-too-widespread abuse of personal human rights in the years since 2001 and the dreadful attacks on New York's Twin Towers and other targets in the United States. Shaker's eventual return to Britain came some several months after Corbyn participated in a cross-party delegation of Members of Parliament who lobbied in Washington for his release. Senator John McCain, the failed Republican Presidential candidate, remarked that he and Corbyn could have some 'interesting' conversations. Corbyn would surely be up for that, because he talks to every one, notwithstanding differing points of view, and, because of his lengthy personal engagement with a wide range of international campaigns, he is well informed.

In November 2014, Corbyn joined with Julian Lewis, Conservative MP for New Forest, in sponsoring the first ever Parliamentary debate at Westminster on the highly influential Agreement between the UK and the USA for Co-operation in the Uses of Atomic Energy for Mutual Defence Purposes, also known as the Mutual Defence Agreement (MDA), signed in 1958. This detailed text, known to few people, governs how the United States and the UK exchange nuclear materials, technology and equipment.

For the first time in more than 50 years, Parliamentarians debated the Agreement, but not its renewal, which fell due at the end of 2014. Do they know the full content of the Agreement? Apparently, in its subsequent additions, the Agreement covers nuclear-armed Trident missiles, which are at the centre of a fierce debate as Corbyn campaigns for the United Kingdom to meet its commitments under the Nuclear Non-Proliferation Treaty and dispense with nuclear weapons. This hugely expensive programme, recently estimated at £167 billion and rising during its lifetime, and this during an era of unprecedented cuts and austerity in public provision, represents extraordinary extravagance on the 'ultimate insurance policy'. Yet the overwhelming majority of states manage perfectly well without any such insurance. How is this so?

Jeremy Corbyn is a great enthusiast for the domestic record of Clement Attlee, whose Labour government established the National Health Service, much of the UK's Welfare State, and built many affordable homes for those recovering from the depredations of the Second World War. He is less enthusiastic about Attlee's foreign policy, and downright critical of his secret decision to spend £200 million on developing nuclear weapons at a time of genuine austerity in Britain.

In addition, in 1949, Attlee accepted an invitation from the United States to sign the founding document of the North Atlantic Treaty Organisation. Not far away, across the Irish Sea, Seán MacBride, the Irish Foreign Minister, was more farsighted in declining the US invitation, saying later:

> '... I regarded NATO as being a rather dangerous military alliance that might involve Europe in another war at more or less the wish of the United States.'

'North American Treaty Organisation' might be a more accurate description. US military hold the senior operational positions within NATO, including Supreme Allied Commander Europe (SACEUR), although the Secretary General, as the public face of the Organisation, has to date been a European male.

NATO is a US-run, nuclear armed, military alliance, serving the priorities of US Grand Strategy, as it is sometimes called. Thus, after the horrors of 9/11, when NATO Secretary General George

Robertson offered the Organisation's assistance to the US, his offer was initially spurned. Later, unfortunately for many people, the US found a substantial, dangerous and often deadly role for NATO in Afghanistan, as the Organisation extends far more widely its theatres of operation.

US Trident missiles form a significant part of NATO's nuclear arsenal. Many of these are deployed on the Royal Navy's four ageing Vanguard class submarines, which the Americans count as part of the US fleet, as Major General (ret'd) Patrick Cordingley recently told us during a television interview. The US Navy also deploys some of its 14 Trident-armed Ohio class submarines in the Atlantic Ocean. In addition, contrary to the requirements of the Nuclear Non-Proliferation Treaty, the US Air Force deploys about 180 modernised B61 gravity nuclear bombs in five European countries (Belgium, Germany, Italy, The Netherlands, Turkey) and engages Poland, Romania and the Baltic states in exercises to enhance its 'non-strategic nuclear posture in Europe', according to the *SIPRI Yearbook 2015*. Trident forms NATO's 'strategic' nuclear posture, although the distinction between 'strategic' and 'non-strategic' conceals dark intent, as all this nuclear firepower still threatens mass death and destruction in Russia, aggravated by US moves to make some of its nuclear weapons lower yield and therefore, in some sense, more 'useable'.

NATO's nuclear armoury is central to what, in the UK, is somewhat misleadingly called 'Trident renewal' or 'replacement'. In fact, it is the submarines rather than the missiles that the UK government wishes to replace. The US is currently modifying the Trident II D5 missiles for deployment in any new submarines to extend their service life beyond 2028 until 2042, by which time Trident will have been operational for more than 50 years.

Meanwhile, in the United States design of the next generation submarine to replace the Trident-armed Ohio class boats is already under way, with construction of a Common Missile Compartment/Advanced Launcher. Known as 'SSBN-X', 12 submarines are envisaged, a reduction of two on the current fleet, with procurement scheduled for 2021, and deployment on patrol starting in 2031. The last of these 12 submarines is planned to remain in service until

2080. How will submarine technology change during this 65-year period?

Trident missiles, in their essentials, are scheduled to continue in service in the US and UK navies for another 25 years or more. The pressing problem for the Royal Navy is the four ageing and increasingly unreliable Vanguard submarines, over which UK governments have been agonising since Tony Blair exchanged letters with George W Bush in 2006, shortly before leaving office. In May 2015, the deteriorating state of at least one of these submarines, and the declining morale of its crew, was highlighted by Able Seaman William McNeilly, in a 12,000 word report (see *Spokesman 129*). In an extended eyewitness commentary, McNeilly recounted his first dive in *HMS Vanguard*:

> *… there was a loud continuous banging heard by everyone. It was down the forward starboard side. The next day in the junior rates mess, I heard people complaining amongst themselves about it being ignored. After all, patrol objective no.1 is to remain undetected, except by forces allocated in direct support. They suspected it might have been the fore-planes. The fore-plane is a control surface that is used to alter the depth of the submarine. There were jokes about the fore-planes being defective throughout the entire submarine …*

AB Mcneilly's disturbing eyewitness report underlines the decrepit state of the four Vanguard class submarines operated by the Royal Navy. For the UK government, the crux of 'Trident replacement' is actually whether to build three or four 'successor' submarines to replace them to carry the also ageing and 'life-extended' Trident missiles and their modified warheads, 'leased' to the UK by the United States.

The four Vanguard class submarines can carry up to 16 Trident II D5 missiles, each armed with up to three warheads, giving a total of up to 48 warheads on the one deployed submarine under the UK's continuous at-sea deterrence (CASD) posture. The warheads have vast explosive power, ranging up to 100 kilotons, although the Stockholm International Peace Research Institute (SIPRI) comments that 'it is believed that a number of them are deployed with only one warhead, possibly with a reduced explosive yield, to increase the flexibility of nuclear targeting options'. Where are these warheads manufactured? In its *Yearbook 2015*, SIPRI states:

> *The warheads are manufactured at the Atomic Weapons Establishment (AWE) Aldermaston, but are believed to be very similar to the US W76 warhead.'* A footnote adds, *'According to some reports, the UK may have been supplied with the US-produced W76-1 nuclear warhead with an improved firing mechanism.*

If the United States is indeed supplying nuclear warheads and components to the United Kingdom, does that not also contravene the provisions of the Nuclear Non-Proliferation Treaty?

Apparently, Trident's current nuclear warhead was first deployed in the early 1990s and, with modifications, is expected to remain in service until the 2040s. Should the three or four new Trident-carrying submarines actually be built for the Royal Navy, can the United States be relied upon to supply suitable missiles and warheads for all of their projected period of service, into the 2040s and beyond? The US has some form in this regard. In 1980, Margaret Thatcher decided to replace US Polaris nuclear missiles with a 'UK variant of the US Trident system', as Commander Robert Green RN (Ret'd) records in his authoritative study, *Security Without Nuclear Deterrence* (Astron Media, Christchurch, 2010; for an updated and revised ebook edition, see www.amazon.com/dp/BOOMFTBUZS). He continues:

> *The UK agreed to purchase Trident I C-4 missiles. The Reagan administration then quickly opted to replace them with the much more accurate and longer-range Trident II D-5, which made it a counter-force weapon, capable of destroying opposing nuclear weapon systems. In 1982, Thatcher had no choice but to accept the D-5 version …*

The Trident D-5 was bigger than the C-4, and changes were required accordingly. What surprises lie in store for the builders and submariners maintaining UK 'successor' submarines in the long haul to the 2040s and beyond?

One thing is certain: nuclear warheads and Trident missiles aboard Royal Navy submarines will be firmly under US control, as General Cordingley emphasised on television. The Royal Navy 'couldn't fire' Trident missiles without US approval, he told his interviewer.

Jeremy Corbyn opposes nuclear weapons and their inherent threat of catastrophic casualties and destruction. In saying he would not 'press the button', were he to become Prime Minister, Corbyn exposes the myth behind the ritual 'nuclear test' of British political leadership. The reality is that no Prime Minister would have to do this, because that dirty work is delegated to the Commanding Officer of the deployed Trident-carrying submarine, exposing one of the weaknesses in this deathly structure.

The Royal Navy Submarine Service currently has two main parts: its four ballistic missile-armed submarines (SSBNs) 'maintaining the nation's strategic nuclear deterrent', and ten nuclear-powered attack submarines (SSNs), 'fast, deep-diving and capable of a wide range of roles', according to the Navy's website.

Seven Astute class attack submarines are planned to replace the four remaining Trafalgar class SSNs, which were designed as 'Cold War' warriors, according to the Navy. Three Astute class SSNs are already operational, with three more at various stages of production at Barrow-in-Furness. All seven will be nuclear powered, and they will be based at Faslane in Scotland. US commentaries such as *Defense Industry Daily* describe submarine manufacture as a 'strategic' industry for the UK. The Royal Navy Submarine Service will endure, with or without replacements for the four Vanguard class SSBNs. Indeed, the Navy may well be better placed to maintain its other roles without the hugely expensive drain on resources to keep Trident operational. Commander Green, responding to AB McNeilly's eyewitness report, argues that the Royal Navy is increasingly 'out of its depth' with Trident, as it struggles with too few skilled personnel, insufficient money for repairs and replacements, and low morale amongst submariners who may prefer a posting in an attack submarine, whose role is more active and interesting (see *Spokesman 129*). Apparently, the Navy has increasing difficulty in securing sufficient young recruits willing to become submariners.

Notwithstanding those difficulties, the Submarine Service will continue to require the services of those people employed in Faslane, as it will those of the submarine designers and builders concentrated in Barrow. In turn, they will continue to require the substantial supply chain of components, materials and parts that go into manufacturing sophisticated, large-scale, nuclear-powered submarines. In this connection, it is notable that the plant in Scotland which supplies specialised steel for submarines is currently under threat of closure.

Without Trident missiles, not only would plans to replace the four Vanguard SSBNs be abandoned. It seems likely that the build programme of the Astute class SSNs would be scaled down, because the current need to assign one SSN to help the deployed SSBN remain undetected would end. If so, Corbyn's proposal for a defence diversification agency is all the more appropriate. This proposal (see below) was made in the context of the defence sector as a whole and 'transitioning away from nuclear weapons'.

These impressions of an internationalist at work focus particularly on Trident because of its salience in the early months of a five-year, fixed-term Parliament, with little prospect of a general election for the Parliament at Westminster before 2020. Jeremy Corbyn brings a refreshingly new perspective to the debate about nuclear weapons, which has been muted for decades. In this, as in diverse other questions, we can rely on him, in Bertrand Russell's phrase, to 'remember your humanity, and forget the rest'.

* * *

The Road to Damascus

It is almost 15 years since the terrible attacks on the United States on what became known as '9/11'. These deadly 'blowback' assaults were perpetrated in the name of Al-Qaeda ('The Base') which, under Osama bin Laden's leadership, had grown out of the mujahideen, Islamic guerrilla fighters who fought against the Soviet Union after the Soviets invaded Afghanistan in December 1979 in an ill-starred attempt to shore up the Communist government there. Zbigniew Brzezinski, Jimmy Carter's National Security Advisor, insists on taking the 'credit' for that pivotal defeat of the Soviet Union.

Fairly swiftly, September 2001 was followed by colossal US bombardments of Afghanistan, and US special forces unsuccessfully pursuing Osama bin Laden. The Taliban retreated, only to reemerge and continue its long campaign for control in Afghanistan. Osama bin Laden was eventually dispatched in Pakistan, in 2011.

Meanwhile, the US, with British support, led an extended war on Iraq, openly declared in March 2003. Iraq Body Count reckons 224,000 people have died in that conflict to date, including some 167,000 civilians. During the weekend of 5/6 December 2015, 94 people were killed, including 54 executions in Mosul, now controlled by Daish (the Arab acronym for *Al-Dawlah Al-Islamiyah fe Al-Iraq wa Al-Sham:* the Islamic State of Iraq and Syria).

Daish specialise in grisly killings and cruelty. They perpetrate deadly terrorist attacks, including at several locations in Paris where, on Friday 13 November, 129 were killed and more than 350 wounded on the night France played Germany at football. Fortunately, a vigilant Muslim security guard prevented greater carnage at the match by stopping a suicide bomber from entering the stadium. Across town, fans of the American band, Eagles of Death Metal, had little chance when 89 of them were killed by two men at The Bataclan in Boulevard Voltaire.

President Hollande declared the attacks an 'act of war' on France by a terrorist army, and vowed a merciless response. He quickly invoked the Treaty of European Union which states that all EU countries have 'an obligation of aid and assistance by all the means in their power' to any member that is the 'victim of armed aggression'. France also drafted a resolution for the United Nations Security Council, which was agreed unanimously a week later, on 20 November 2015. It called upon:

Member States that have the capacity to do so to take all necessary measures, in compliance with international law, in particular with the United Nations Charter, as well as international human rights, refugee and humanitarian law, on the territory under the control of ISIL also known as Da'esh, in Syria and Iraq, to redouble and coordinate their efforts to prevent and suppress terrorist acts committed specifically by ISIL also known as Da'esh as well as ANF [Al-Nusrah Front], and all other individuals, groups, undertakings, and entities associated with Al-Qaida, and other terrorist groups, as designated by the United Nations Security Council, and as may further be agreed by the International Syria Support Group (ISSG) and endorsed by the UN Security Council, pursuant to the statement of the International Syria Support Group (ISSG) of 14 November, and to eradicate the safe haven they have established over significant parts of Iraq and Syria;

The 44-minute meeting of the Security Council was chaired by Matthew Rycroft, British Permanent Representative to the United Nations. In July 2002, Rycroft wrote for 'UK EYES ONLY' the notorious 'Downing Street Memo' which recorded the head of the Secret Intelligence Service reporting on his recent talks in Washington:

> *There was a perceptible shift in attitude. Military action was now seen as inevitable. Bush wanted to remove Saddam, through military action, justified by the conjunction of terrorism and weapons of mass destruction (WMD). But the intelligence and facts were being fixed around the policy. The National Security Council (NSC) had no patience with the UN route, and no enthusiasm for publishing material on the Iraqi regime's record. There was little discussion in Washington of the aftermath after military action.*

After the first of three unanimous votes in the Security Council, David Cameron, British Prime Minister, saw his best chance of reversing the humiliating defeat of 2013, when the House of Commons voted not to authorise use of UK military force against President Assad's Syria, following chemical weapon attacks on Ghouta, a suburb of Damascus, in which many people died. These dreadful events are still under scrutiny by the Organisation for the Prohibition of Chemical Weapons. Nevertheless, the UK's pause in the rush to war on Syria gave time for President Obama to have second thoughts and, subsequently, Russia with others pursued the chemical disarmament of Syria under the UN Chemical Weapons Convention.

Two years later, with an overall majority of twelve in the House of Commons, buttressed by the UN resolution in the wake of the Paris attacks, Cameron felt sufficiently sure of his ground to seek a vote to endorse his intention to join in the aerial bombardment of Syria led by the United States. In the event, the House voted almost two to one in support of the Government motion, to support

> *Her Majesty's government in taking military action, specifically airstrikes, exclusively against Isil in Syria.*

Jeremy Corbyn allowed a free vote among Labour Members of Parliament, and 66 voted with the Government. David Cameron whipped his Conservative Party, but 14 Tories nevertheless defied their leader. Seven voted for the amendment, in the name of Conservative MP John Baron, which stated that the House

does not believe that the case for the UK's participation in the ongoing air campaign in Syria by 10 countries has been made under current circumstances, and consequently declines to authorise military action in Syria.

Seven more abstained, including Kenneth Clarke, John Redwood and Edward Leigh. These 14 represented a sizeable rebellion against the Government which exceeds by two its slender overall majority in the House. More significantly, the interventions by some of these Tory dissidents got closer to the truth of the matter. Julian Lewis, Chair of the Defence Committee, consulted the journalist Patrick Cockburn, based in the region, about the Joint Intelligence Committee's claim that some 70,000 'moderate' fighters might join the fight against Daish. Cockburn replied:

'Unfortunately, the belief that there are 70,000 moderate opposition fighters on the ground in Syria is wishful thinking. The armed opposition is dominated by Isis or al-Qaeda type organisations. There are many small and highly fragmented groups of opposition fighters who do not like Assad or Isis and could be described as non-extremist, but they are generally men from a single clan, tribe or village. They are often guns for hire and operate under licence from the al-Qaeda affiliate, the al-Nusra Front, or its near equivalent, Ahrar al-Sham. Many of these groups seek to present a moderate face abroad but remain violently sectarian and intolerant inside Syria.'

Dr Lewis also consulted the UK's former ambassador to Syria, Peter Ford, who described the Free Syrian Army as:

'a ragbag of 58 factions (at the last count) united mainly by a desire to use the FSA appellation in order to secure Gulf, Turkish and Western funding … most of the factions, which are extremely locally based, have no interest whatsoever in being drawn into battles against groups which basically share their sectarian agenda hundreds of miles away in areas with which they are unfamiliar.'

As Dr Lewis remarked to the House, 'instead of having dodgy dossiers we now have bogus battalions of moderate fighters'. He concluded:

Airstrikes alone are a dangerous diversion and distraction. What is needed is a grand military alliance involving not only the west but Russia and, yes, its Syrian Government clients too.

Syria's dreadful and prolonged war risks becoming a proxy war between Russia, with Iran and China, on one side, and the United States and its allies on the other. This is in addition to the proxy conflict between Kurds and Turks, and sundry other local hostilities. Strategic interests are at stake, including rival pipelines to bring natural gas to international markets.

NATO perceives as a threat the Russian airbase at Latakia in northern Syria, close to the Turkish border. So it was that Turkish F-16s shot down an ageing Russian aircraft as it returned from bombing predominantly Turkmen villages close to the border. This calculated act, exacerbated by killing the Russian pilot as he parachuted to earth and a Russian soldier sent to rescue his compatriots, has drawn an icy response from President Putin. He will calculate his response. The world holds its breath whilst the next escalation of this combustible conflict smoulders.

In the early 1980s, when he was Deputy Leader of the Labour Party, the late Denis Healey used to worry publicly about the risks of conflict spreading that were inherent in the Iraq-Iran war. Iraq declared war on Iran in September 1980, a year or so after the Islamic Revolution overthrew the Shah. Saddam had the support of the West in this misadventure, which included attacks with chemical weapons, manufactured in plants constructed with help from Western companies, as Robin Cook remarked when he resigned from Tony Blair's Government to oppose the then Prime Minister's war on Iraq, in 2003. The Iraq-Iran war lasted for eight long years, with more than 500,000 people dead and widespread destruction. A ceasefire was finally brokered through the United Nations in 1988. Healey's worry was how one war seeds another, and that has certainly come to pass in the Middle East.

Jeremy Corbyn seemed to have in mind similar concerns when he spoke in the truncated debate on Syria. He had pressed for a two-day debate so that all those who wished to speak would have an opportunity to do so. But the Prime Minister was in a hurry and, within hours of the vote, the RAF was bombing targets in Syria which, according to US sources, had already been bombed more than once. Corbyn, reflecting widespread public scepticism about raining down more expensive bombs on Syria, said:

> *It is impossible to avoid the conclusion that the Prime Minister understands that public opinion is moving increasingly against what I believe to be an ill-thought-out rush to war. He wants to hold this vote before opinion against it grows even further. Whether it is a lack of strategy worth the name, the absence of credible ground troops, the missing diplomatic plan for a Syrian settlement, the failure to address the impact of the terrorist threat or the refugee crisis and civilian casualties, it is becoming increasingly clear that the Prime Minister's proposals for military action simply do not stack up.*

Corbyn emphasised that

> *the Prime Minister has avoided spelling out to the British people the warnings that he has surely been given about the likely impact of UK air strikes in Syria on the threat of terrorist attacks in the UK.*

The Leader of the Opposition reflected on the period since 9/11:

> *In the past week, voice has been given to the growing opposition to the Government's bombing plans – across the country, in Parliament, outside in the media, and indeed in my own party. I believe that this is in consideration of all the wars that we have been involved in over the last 14 years. These matters were debated a great deal during my campaign to be elected leader of the Labour party, and many people think very deeply about these matters. In the light of that record of western military interventions, these matters have to be analysed. British bombing in Syria risks yet more of what President Obama, in a very thoughtful moment, called the "unintended consequences" of the war in Iraq, which he himself opposed at the time. The spectre of Iraq, Afghanistan and Libya looms over this debate.*

Mr Corbyn concluded:

> *To oppose another war and intervention is not pacifism; it is hard-headed common sense. That is what we should be thinking about today in the House. To resist ISIL's determination to draw the western powers back into the heart of the Middle East is not to turn our backs on allies; it is to refuse to play into the hands of ISIL as I suspect some of its members want us to. Is it wrong for us here in Westminster to see a problem, pass a motion, and drop bombs, pretending we are doing something to solve it? That is what we did in Afghanistan, Iraq and Libya.*

Has terrorism increased or decreased as a result of all that? The Prime Minister said he was looking to build a consensus around the military action he wants to take. I do not believe he has achieved anything of the kind. He has failed, in my view, to make the case for another bombing campaign.

The House disagreed, but many outside think otherwise. Now the UK is again at war, and Mr Cameron urges patience, that it will take three years or so. In this, he echoes John Kerry, the US Secretary of State, who is also guessing about the timeline. Mr Kerry will likely have departed office by 2018. Will Mr Cameron also have walked, dragged down by another inept and deadly intervention in the Middle East? Or will the diplomatic push for a partial ceasefire at last bring some relief to the long-suffering people of Syria?

11

Socialist Renewal and Workers' Control

Tom Unterrainer

Our values do not change. Our commitment to a different vision of society stands intact. But the ways of achieving that vision must change. The programme we are in the process of constructing entirely reflects our values. Its objectives would be instantly recognizable to our founders.[1]

Tony Blair, 1997

Blair and New Labour did not kill the Labour Party and did not finish off socialism. History has not fully caught up with Tony Blair, but it is fair to say that the processes of retribution are well under way. One startling aspect of this 'retribution' is the magnificent and frankly startling election of Jeremy Corbyn as Labour's new leader. Jeremy's election has unleashed an organisational frenzy in the grass roots of the Labour Party and has opened up a unique opportunity for the renewal of British socialism. Any renewal will necessitate reclaiming the values, vision and objectives of the socialist project.

Ken Coates identified the 'morality' of British socialism as being 'captured in two very simple slogans: "Do as you would be done by", as Charles Kingsley insisted, and, in the words of William Morris: "No man is good enough to be another man's master"'.[2] These slogans, relating to the principles of equality and freedom respectively, must surely retain their place at the heart of any definition of socialism, in Britain and beyond. Uniting these aims must be central to the socialist idea. Yet we live in a world where such moral aspirations seem more unachievable than ever: we reside in a Britain where 'do as you would be done by' has more than a sniff of pulpit abstraction about it; where the idea that 'no person is good enough to be another's master' seems equally abstract.

What are the causes of this 'abstractedness'? Socialism and the institutions and organisations that traditionally incubated and projected socialist ideas have either been entrenched in defensive manoeuvres for decades or, as with the Labour Party under Blair, encumbered with a leadership with no regard for socialism. Socialism appears to have been re-defined through an interacting process of defensive necessity and a lack of dynamism into a series of 'what-we're-against-isms'. There are obvious exceptions to this generalisation, where small groups of socialists have mobilised thousands – and on occasion, millions[3] – to resist the drives to war and austerity. But it seems reasonable to assume that these socialists are aware of the road yet to be travelled by specifically socialist ideas. In any case, a 'socialist movement' cannot be reduced to the exceptional talents of individual socialists or very small groups of them.

The move to defensiveness is itself a product of the failure to halt, reverse and make good the manifold attacks, set-backs and betrayals that working people have experienced at the hands of rampant, neoliberal capitalism. The impact of neoliberalism on the practice of successive British governments can perhaps be best defined as a sustained and concrete move towards making Britain – its social organisation, institutions and economy – as attractive a place as possible for global capital to 'do business'. In this context, the space for genuine and extensive social reform is very narrow indeed. This reality, together with the willing acquiescence of social democratic parties across Europe to the imperatives of neoliberalism, has fuelled a crisis in the traditional political organisations of the working class.

In his 1988 essay 'British Socialism – into the Twenty-First Century', Ken Coates claimed that whilst '"Do as you would be done by" is still a good motto, none of us can live up to it'. This claim is as valid today as it was almost thirty years ago, perhaps more so. Across the whole of British society inequalities have sharpened and become entrenched as the engines of unfettered accumulation, neoliberal restructuring and austerity have ground on. In housing, unemployment, public health and education we can see how walls have been raised between and through large swathes of society. If we consider just one aspect of the divisions engendered by inequality – in the workplace – it may be possible to illustrate the core problems we face and the possibilities for articulating a solution.

Can the manager of a small convenience store 'do as she would be done by' when calling in shop workers, employed on zero-hours contracts, at an hours' notice to fill a staffing rota? Can the area manager – probably employed on a close-to-median wage – whose contract is stuffed with unachievable targets, be expected to exchange pleasantries or express any understanding with the shop manager – employed on just above the minimum wage – when it's imperative that an online tracking system be fed with information to account for missed sales targets?

What about the call-centre workers? Can the twenty-two year old graduate – one of those faceless potential saviours we all rely upon from time-to-time – with £30,000 debt and rent-arrears really be expected to express sympathy when your broadband malfunctions? Can the call-centre 'supervisor', whose toilet breaks are monitored by a computer system (just like everyone else), be called upon to 'do as she would be done by' as she listens in and rates the quality of calls?

The organisation of modern capitalism and the multiple deformations and degradations of work – some old, some new – leaves very little space for 'do as you would be done by' to operate. This fact is readily observable within the types of workplace described above, but it is equally evident if the stratification between types of work and different workplaces is considered. For example, the differences are stark between the working conditions and the 'experiences of work' subjected on a highly unionised workforce such as teachers, on the one hand, and those employed on minimum wage, zero hours contracts in a variety of industries, on the other. It is unquestionably the case that teachers' working conditions have suffered multiple and sustained attacks from successive governments and that to a large extent the teaching profession 'isn't what it was'. However, it is also true that, after thirty years or more of sustained warfare and at least fifteen years of acute attacks upon the teaching profession, teachers still have recognisable contracts; working conditions; trade union representation; pensions and so forth. That is, something approximating to 'standard' industrial relations still exists. This is not the case for the growing band of working people employed on a basis more closely resembling Victorian conditions than anything witnessed in the late 20th or early 21st centuries. Unite the Union's campaign to expose the employment practices of Sports Direct is a case in point. The union describes this firm as employing 'a zero hours contract workforce in constant fear of losing their jobs with staff named and shamed over a Tannoy for not working fast enough'.[4]

There is very little discernible equality between the two groups of workers described here. The cavernous gap between the degraded industrial relations governing the working lives of teachers, and the complete lack of identifiable modern industrial relations for the Sport Direct workers, implies not only a very different work experience but also a very different experience of life itself. Closing this gap is an important element in pursuing a renewal for socialism as a living, breathing entity, but simple policy changes will not suffice in achieving equality in the workplace.

Peter Fleming provides some stark evidence for the argument that the *organisation* of work under neoliberal capitalism is only one part of the problem. For example:

> *When a 21-year-old banking intern, Moritz Erhardt, died in his London apartment in 2013, it attracted worldwide attention. What was so troubling about his death was that it followed 72 straight hours of stressful work. Subsequent reports pointed to an industry mentality that gleefully celebrated such arduous displays of commitment. Working incredibly long hours is a badge of honour, something to be proud of and rewarded by the company. Erdhardt's parents stated that they had become increasingly worried about their son's lifestyle, noting how his emails were sent at very unusual times, indicating that he was working too much.[5]*

'Working too much' may sound like a facile complaint in an era where the aspiration of a full-employment economy is barely addressed by policy makers. All the more so when the example of a banking intern – someone who could reasonably expect a six-figure salary in times to come – is invoked to illustrate the problem. But what Fleming is pointing to, and what he is absolutely right to place as a central consideration in analysing work in the twenty-first century, is the grotesquely exaggerated place that work occupies in the human experience. Work, and working hard, is seen to validate our lives, to give meaning and purpose to our waking hours. Hard work makes us 'better' people. If our work is all consuming then, logic suggests, we are on the right track. Conversely, those who are unable to work for whatever reason are considered somehow 'less than human'.

The all-consuming nature of work is not simply a matter of hours worked, but of the stresses and strains embedded into the modern workplace. Work organisation has always involved monitoring, targets and appraisals in one form or another, but modern work organisation has harnessed new technologies to intensify these processes to an exponential degree. Whereas in the past such processes were mediated through another person, opening up the possibilities for the exercising of 'human judgement' and good sense, we are now at the mercy of faceless algorithms, spreadsheets and automated processes.

Not only does this increasing tendency to lack of autonomy at work lead to ill health, but it also edges out opportunities to live fully human lives. This is not an especially new phenomenon, as Ken Coates made clear in his 1988 essay:

> *If we have begun to recognize that it is deeply wrong to expose people to workplaces in which conditions render them deaf, or lame, is it not equally wrong to expose them to a mechanical existence in which their hours and years are simply eaten away, offering nothing but money in return, leaving them only a husk of leisure time in which to live as creative, developing and loving people?*[6]

Bertrand Russell noted something similar, in 1919, when considering what a free human existence would look like:

> *In the world which we should wish to see, there will be more joy of life than in the drab tragedy of modern everyday existence ... [where] most men are bowed down by forethought, no longer capable of light-hearted gaiety, but only of a kind of solemn jollification by the clock at the appropriate hours.*[7]

A socialism uncoupled from the aim of full human liberation is not worthy of the name. Ending inequality within and between workplaces and society at large is an urgent task. It will require forensic examination of the nature of work today and the ways in which work organisation in the age of neoliberalism has extended out of the workplace. But the question of equality, and the consideration it has been given here, is only one part of 'definition' of the morality of socialism that we are attempting to deal with. The other – 'no person is good enough to be another's master' – cannot be discarded, and neither can the two be separated, for:

> … *if the combination of goals is not easy, their separation leads us in the wrong direction. Equality without freedom will inhibit creativity, but freedom without equality will produce the subjugation and the domination of some people by others. Socialism is a continuing and difficult search to find the best possible relationship between what can easily be, and usually are, incompatible commitments. The best that is possible in one generation, at one level of knowledge and technique, will not necessarily be the best for its successors. That is why one generation cannot bind another, and why the political process must remain open and accountable. Part of this openness requires that we see the continuing struggle against inequalities as a process of widening personal freedoms in concerned joint action. Such freedoms cannot easily be handed down by lawgivers because their exercise is a key part of the work involved in establishing them. Legislators can unlock the barriers to freedom, but without people ready and able to enjoy it, it will be uneasily established.*[8]

If we take Morris's dictum seriously – as we undoubtedly should – and focus in on Coates' insistence that '[s]uch freedoms cannot easily be handed down', the question of overcoming domination 'from above' and replacing it with the exercise of individual and collective freedoms 'from below' seems to be a complex one. However, there is good reason to believe that such a re-balancing of power is a distinct possibility. This is because the notion of 'control' – who has it and how it is used – has been fundamental to trade union organisation and practice throughout the history of the movement. Indeed, the very first union-type organisations focused on controlling and regulating not only terms and conditions of employment but also the supply of labour into certain 'crafts'.

In the 1890s, the first two instances of industrial action taken by the National Union of Teachers, for example, featured elements of workers' control. During the disputes themselves local Associations of the Union were able to mount successful strike action by preventing the flow of scab labour into the affected areas.

'On 22 February 1896 four certified male assistant teachers were dismissed from Highland Road School for failing to arrive at school at the agreed starting time of 7.55 a.m.'[9] This seemingly drastic action followed a demand from the Portsmouth and District Teachers' Association (the local affiliate to the National Union) to the Portsmouth School Board demanding comparable pay to teachers in neighbouring school boards. When members of the School Board attempted to transfer three teachers from another school to Highland Road, these teachers refused and were promptly locked out of their original schools. Local Associations across the country recognised the importance of this action and mobilised to prevent teachers from elsewhere being brought in to break the strike.

The context of this action in Portsmouth, and the response of Teacher Associations nationally, was the attempt to control who entered the teaching profession – including advocating the need for proper training and 'certification' – and an attempt to secure a national framework of pay and conditions for the profession.

A similar pattern of events and responses unfolded in West Ham, in 1907, where teacher unions took control of labour supply – to such an extent that the Aldermen of West Ham attempted to bring teachers from Scotland to break the strike.

In such circumstances, 'workers' control' is not synonymous with 'the workers taking over' or 'revolution', but has a specific and important character as an emblem of effective labour movement organisation.

The definition offered by Carter L. Goodrich[10] in 1920 of 'the fighting frontier of control' is a vital departure point for the sort of 'thinking and action' that now seems vital if we are to restore effective and democratic organisation in the workplace:

> *"Workers' control" is, I suppose, often translated as "interfering with the employers' business." A definite notion of the meaning attached to the latter phrase would be of use in finding the fighting frontier of control. Where does this issue come out into the open? At what point does the employer say – beyond this there shall be no discussion, the rest is my business alone? The line is a hard one to draw; the issues are rarely thought out in the abstract and rarely presented dramatically. The real frontier, like most lines in industry, is more a matter of accepted custom than of precisely stated principle. In a few instances, however, there have been definite attempts to stake out the boundary, evidently as results of disputes in which the principle became explicit.[11]*

Locating the 'fighting frontier of control' and testing its boundaries on a planned basis should be an essential component in reviving our movement.

Referring again to the issues facing teachers and their unions, exactly what 'testing the boundaries' of the frontier of control might mean can be elaborated somewhat.

Neoliberalism has dramatically 're-made' the education landscape. There has been a proliferation of privately-owned (as companies limited by guarantee) and publicly-funded academies and 'free schools', which are steadily replacing community and comprehensive schools. This process can be seen as part of neoliberalism's drive towards deregulating sectors of the economy 'formerly run or regulated by the state'.[12] In a global economy, where education is one of the last significant but largely untapped markets, it is easy to see the material drivers for such a process.

As the 'governance' of schools – what they do and the mechanisms for doing it – shifts from the national and local level to the individual academy level (or, increasingly, to the 'academy chain' level), a settled regime of 'governance' is as yet absent. It is very much the case that certain academy operators are 'trying their luck' in terms of terms and conditions of employment, but a great deal of custom-and-practice has been retained. However, in tandem with deregulating the school sector, central government has been 'reforming' aspects of law governing the terms and conditions of employment of teachers on the national scale. The most notable feature of this is the introduction of performance-related pay for teachers, although the changes are in fact legion. So there is a dual pressure on teachers and, as such, two forces acting to significantly deform (or 'reform' in the official language) the nature of teachers' work.

Dramatic changes to the nature of teachers' work have been noted[13]: 'flexible post-Fordist forms of production and restructured workplace organization'; 'a greater reliance on market forces as a mode of regulation', and 'a re-centralization of control in contexts where responsibility for meeting production targets is devolved' (where 'production' refers to the tasks undertaken by teachers when they 'teach'). Smyth and colleagues note that:

We are experiencing a dramatic shift in the boundaries of control from direct, overt and bureaucratic form of surveillance, to much more covert forms that take expression in the nature of the way in which work itself is being restructured.[14]

As a consequence, changes that seem outrageous in the extreme to some experienced teachers and critical researchers have become 'normalised', to a certain extent, within the teaching workforce.

Central to these 'covert' forms of managerial control is the process by which a separation between the 'conception and execution' of teachers' tasks is taking place.[15] An increasingly small number of people within the teaching workforce make decisions about what is taught, how and when, whilst the vast majority are expected to carry out such decisions without question. This process has the following features:

the increasingly complex division of labour within the education workforce and labour substitution; the intensification of teachers' work; and the growth of management hierarchies as a mechanism of control designed to further drive up 'output' as measured by student achievement.[16]

As yet, there are no in-depth studies into the effect of the introduction of performance-related pay for teachers on the processes described. However, it seems reasonable to assume that such a policy has significantly shifted the line at which management within a single school feels empowered to declare 'beyond this there will be no discussion'. As such, systems of management control – some new, others a legacy from the 'good old days' of school organisation – have been strengthened, and the frontier of control in schools has shifted in management's favour.

If these processes are to be either contested or arrested, in schools and other workplaces, then the 'spirit' of workers' control needs to be revived.

Ken Coates and Tony Topham give a very clear definition of what this 'spirit' will involve:

'Workers' control' emphasises that the purpose of the policy and strategy should be to establish control, by workers, over the hitherto unfettered decisions of the ruling party in industry, namely the employers and their managers. In this sense … the germs of workers' control exist, in greater or lesser degree, wherever strong

independent trade-union and shop-floor powers act to restrain employers in the exercise of their so-called 'prerogatives'.[17]

Whilst the 'germs' are very much in place in workplaces such as schools – which have the advantage of high levels of unionisation – it goes without saying that teachers and their unions are some way from establishing rigorous and systematic approaches to workers' control. In workplaces and industries that lack the levels of representation seen in schools and some other sections of the public sector, the notion of workers' control could be used to start a process of building and rebuilding workplace organisation.

How do these two 'bygone' mottoes, and the implications of taking them seriously, relate to the dramatic shifts unleashed by Jeremy Corbyn's victory? Both encapsulate an antidote to the spin most starkly evident in a comparison between Tony Blair's assertions quoted at the start of this argument and the realities of New Labour's political practice. Blairism constituted a fundamental breach, not only with the values articulated and fought for by the founders of the Labour Party, but also with the millions who have passed through its ranks in search of socialist answers to the degradations of capitalism.

Jeremy Corbyn's victory has not yet undone all the damage rendered on the Labour Party and society at large by the New Labour experience. What his victory has achieved is a closing of the fundamental rupture brought about by Blairism between the Labour Party's leadership and the mass movements outside of Parliament.

Jeremy Corbyn's victory would not have been possible without the mobilisation of tens of thousands of activists, initiative-takers and organisers – not all of whom knew they were such people before the start of the campaign. This development is vital if we are to have any hope of reviving the 'morality' of British socialism.

A more free and equal society – in the sense discussed here – will not come about through legislation alone because any renewal of socialism will require an expansive, dynamic and interacting democratic process to be unleashed. In Britain, the main historical drivers of this process have been the trade unions and associated organisations. In the post-war period, every major change in the political life of this country emerged not from the depths of Parliament but from concerted, extra-Parliamentary action by the unions.

For sure, legislation is required to remove the barriers that have been built up over generations that currently stifle our efforts, and it is equally true that a programme of emergency legislation could work to improve the lives of millions in fairly short order. The immediate repeal of anti-trade union laws and invasive surveillance legislation, for example, would be very useful legislative measures in terms of granting greater freedoms. A prospective government committed to implementing a real living wage, re-building the welfare state, and reversing the privatisation of the NHS would make great strides towards a more equal society. We should all expect to see such legislation if Jeremy Corbyn forms a Labour government in the future. We should also expect to see a dynamic, grass-roots movement wielding considerable influence on the course of events. For, as Ken Coates noted:

> *The basic personal right which is rejected by modern dictators is the right to join up with other people in voluntary associations of every kind. The right to organize to achieve whatever objectives one sets oneself, is the right to lobby and negotiate for change. In advanced democracies, governments would not only recognize but encourage such associations. They would invite them to participate to join in solving social problems and they would see them as a valuable social resource.*[18]

That grass-roots, mass movement will be the vital factor on the path to meeting the challenges articulated by 'Do as you would be done by' and 'No man is good enough to be another man's master' in all their possible forms. Its work will be to mobilise and organise the extension of social freedoms and democratic control across British society; to ensure that a future Labour Government reacts to and protects these freedoms in legislative terms; to build links with socialist and trade union movements throughout Europe and beyond because the renewal of socialism in Britain is inseparable from and dependent upon processes unfolding on an international scale.

Now is a time to experiment, to be bold, to listen, to discuss and to join together in concerted action. If we miss this opportunity or fail to recognise it as such, then we will miss a chance to take steps toward the fundamental social transformation of society. Such chances are too rare to miss.

Notes

11. Blair, Tony (1997), *New Britain: My Vision of a Young Country*, Fourth Estate, London.
12. Coates, Ken (1988), 'British Socialism – into the Twenty-First Century', *Socialism 21*, Spokesman, Nottingham.
13. I'm thinking here of the core groups responsible for the Stop the War Coalition and the People's Assembly.
14. Retrieved from www.unitetheunion.org/news/unite-launches-campaign-to-tackle-victorian-work-practices-in-sports-direct
15. Fleming, Peter (2015), *The Mythology of Work: How capitalism persists despite itself*, Pluto, London, pp 49.
16. Coates, Ken (1988), 'British Socialism – into the Twenty-First Century', *Socialism 21*, Spokesman, Nottingham.
17. Russell, Bertrand (1919), *Proposed Roads to Freedom*, Spokesman, Nottingham.
18. Coates, Ken (1988), 'British Socialism – into the Twenty-First Century', *Socialism 21*, Spokesman, Nottingham.
19. Seifert, Roger V. (1987), *Teacher Militancy: A History of Teacher Strikes 1896-1987*, The Falmer Press: Lewes
10. Goodrich, Carter L. (1975), *The Frontier of Control: A Study in British Workshop Politics*, Pluto: London
11. Ibid, pp56
12. Harvey, David (2005) *A Brief History of Neoliberalism*, OUP: Oxford
13. myth, J et al (2000), *Teachers' Work in a Globalizing Economy*, Falmer Press: London
14. Ibid
15. Labour Process Theory is an essential tool for studying the changing nature of work in any environment. The central ideas are comprehensively articulated in Braverman, Harry (1974) *Labor and Monopoly Capital: the Degradation of Work in the Twentieth Century*, Monthly Review Press: New York.
16. Carter, Bob and Stevenson, Howard (2012) 'Teachers, workforce remodelling and the challenge to labour process analysis', *Work, Employment & Society* 26:481
17. Coates, Ken and Topham, Tony (1974), *The New Unionism: The Case for Workers' Control*, Pelican: London
18. Coates, Ken (1988), 'British Socialism – into the Twenty-First Century', *Socialism 21*, Spokesman, Nottingham.

Appendices
Campaign Policies

These policy statements were issued in summer 2015, during Jeremy Corbyn's successful campaign for election as leader of the Labour Party.

I
The Economy in 2020

Issued 22 July 2015

Wealth creation is a good thing: we all want greater prosperity. But let us have a serious debate about how wealth is created. If you believe the Conservative myth then wealth creation is solely due to the dynamic risk-taking of private equity funds, entrepreneurs or billionaires bringing their investment to UK shores.

So if we follow the Conservatives' tale then it is logical to cut taxes for the rich and big business, not to bother to invest in the workforce, and be intensely relaxed about the running down of public services. But in reality wealth creation is a collective process between workers, public investment and services, and, yes, often innovative and creative individuals. Understanding this means getting to grips with the key choice in the leadership election and indeed the key choice facing Britain: Whether to accept austerity or whether to break free of this straitjacket and strike out for a modern, rebalanced economy based on growth and high quality jobs.

Labour must create a balanced economy that ensures workers and government share fairly in the wealth creation process

● that encourages and supports innovation in every sector of the economy; and
● that invests in skills and infrastructure to build an economy that is more sustainable and more equal.

The purpose of this document is to set out some of the key parts of that vision. That includes not only the overall approach we must take to the economy as a whole, but some specific key changes on taxation.

The budget and austerity

George Osborne's post-election Budget speech was praised as a slick piece of political manoeuvring. His political trick on the minimum wage was exposed within hours, but it was an attempt to outflank the too-modest-by-far plan that Labour had for £8 per hour by 2020. Some of us had been pushing for a genuine living wage. The TUC calls for £10 per hour.

But look deeper at Osborne's Budget and a familiar story emerges: tax cuts at the top. This time for the 4% who currently pay inheritance tax, and then for corporations again. And who bears the brunt? Once again it's low income families, disabled people, young people, public sector workers, and our public services. So we see that austerity is about political choices, not economic necessities.

There is money available: the inheritance tax changes will lose the government over £2.5 billion in revenue between now and 2020. What responsible government committed to closing the deficit would give a tax break to the richest 4% of households? The Conservatives are giving away to the very rich twice as much as reducing the benefit cap will raise by further impoverishing the poorest.

Another choice was to cut corporation tax – already the lowest in the G7 at 20%. Lower too than the 25% in China, and half the 40% rate in the United States. That political choice will see our revenue intake from big business fall by £2.5 billion in 2020. That's nearly twice the amount saved by cutting child tax credits beyond two children.

So closing the deficit and austerity are just the cover for the same old Conservative policies: run down public services, slash the welfare state, sell off public assets and give tax cuts to the wealthiest. This is why I stood in this race: Because Labour shouldn't be swallowing the story that austerity is anything other than a new facade for the same Tory plans.

We all want the deficit closed on the current budget, but there was no need to try to do it within an artificial five years or even the extra five years George Osborne mapped out two weeks ago. As I said on the Sunday Politics, if the deficit has been closed by 2020 and the economy is growing, then Labour should not run a current budget deficit – but we should borrow to invest in our future prosperity.

You don't close the deficit fairly or sustainably through cuts. You close it through growing a balanced and sustainable economy that works for all. And by asking those with income and wealth to spare to contribute more.

Deficit, growth, investment

If Osborne's forecasts are right there won't be a deficit by 2020, but if – like last time – he is proved wrong and he only again manages to halve the deficit then I make this pledge:

Labour will close the current budget deficit through building a strong growing economy that works for all. We will not do it by increasing poverty. The discussion about the deficit leads us to the clearest possible choice.

Rather than remove spending power from the economy and damage growth and future prosperity, Britain needs a publicly-led expansion and reconstruction of the economy. We must put this centre-stage as the alternative to the current model of austerity for the poor, and deregulation, privatisation and never-ending corporate tax sweeteners for the super-rich and big business.

We need a fairer system for all, including on taxation, which I will set out here. To date, we have seen only the most feeble of upturns:

● We have had the longest period of falling real wages since the 19th century
● A disastrous investment and productivity record
● A swelling balance of payments deficit
● The creation of an army of low-paid, low skill, insecure, zero hours, bogus self-employment jobs.

People are still worse off today than they were in 2008. The average household is still awaiting recovery. So to deliver rising living standards and decent jobs for the majority – which has got to be the focus of any Labour programme – we need a strategy for faster, more sustainable growth, as well as policies – including on taxation – to make sure that growth is more fairly distributed.

But as a principle to create the kind of economy we need, Britain needs sharply rising levels of investment in the economy. Faster growth and higher wages must be key to bringing down the deficit. Increased tax receipts and lower benefit demand are a better way forward than shutting local libraries and attacking the working poor.

If there are tough choices, we will always protect public services and support for the most vulnerable. Instead we will ask those who have been fortunate to contribute a little more. With a sustainable investment plan, we can ensure more people fall into that fortunate category too.

An economy that works for all

But our economy remains fundamentally unbalanced. Large parts of our country have been neglected for decades, with no real industrial strategy. The Northern Powerhouse is largely southern hot air: it devolves only already slashed budgets, leaving the real levers centralised and unused. Our national infrastructure – energy, housing, transport, digital – is outdated, leaving the UK lagging behind other developed economies.

There was nothing in the Budget about boosting public investment, in fact the Budget data shows it will be cut back even further. You cannot cut your way to prosperity. We need to invest in our future. A strategic state cannot leave our infrastructure to deregulated privatised markets. They are failing people and holding back our economy.

Modern housing, transport, digital and energy networks are the foundation stone of a modern economy, and we need to ensure they are among the best in the world. Public investment in new publicly-owned infrastructure so that a future chancellor can deliver a sound economy, not just sound-bites. We need to drive investment and lending to reshape and rebuild the economy: Focused on hi-tech and innovation and the infrastructure to support that, rebuilding supply chains to stimulate private sector demand. The 'rebalancing' I have talked about here means rebalancing away from finance towards the high-growth, sustainable sectors of the future.

How do we do this? One option would be for the Bank of England to be given a new mandate to upgrade our economy to invest in new large scale housing, energy, transport and digital pro-jects: quantitative easing for people instead of banks. Richard Murphy has been one of many economists making that case.

Another option would be to strip out some of the huge tax reliefs and subsidies on offer to the corporate sector. These amount to £93 billion a year – money which would be better used in direct public investment, which in turn would give a stimulus to private sector supply chains.

These funds could be used to establish a 'National Investment Bank' to invest in the new infrastructure we need and in the hi-tech and innovative industries of the future.

To invest in infrastructure also requires a clear strategy in the construction, manufacturing, and engineering skills to build and maintain that new infrastructure so vital to sustainable economic growth.

So taking this approach, in the coming days this campaign will set out how we propose to invest in adult education and further education more generally to get the high skill, high pay, high productivity workforce we all want – building on our announcements already on university education.

Taxation

The biggest issue facing British politics right now is not whether the top rate of tax should be 45% or 50%, or whether corporation tax should be 18% or 20%. The big question is how to get some of the wealthiest individuals and biggest corporations to pay anything like their fair share. At a time when schools and hospitals are struggling for funds, it is grotesque that some of the richest individuals and most profitable businesses are dodging their responsibilities.

Paying tax is not a burden. It is the subscription we pay to live in a civilised society. A collective payment we all make for the collective goods we all benefit from: schools, hospitals, libraries, street lights, pensions, the list is endless.

Our tax system has shifted over the last generation from taxing income and wealth to taxing consumption; and from taxing corporations to taxing individuals.These changes have helped to make our society more unequal and our tax system more regressive.

So I make this pledge: Labour must make the tax system more progressive: ensuring that those with the most pay the most, not just in monetary terms, but proportionally too.

Tax justice
But whatever tax laws we pass, we won't get a progressive tax system in reality unless we can enforce it and collect the tax we are owed. A detailed analysis last year produced by Richard Murphy suggests that the government is missing out on nearly £120 billion in tax revenues, per year. That's enough to double the NHS budget; enough to give every man, woman and child in this country £2,000. The £120bn figure is made up from:

● about £20bn in tax debt, uncollected by HMRC which continues to suffer budget and staffing cuts (only partially reversed in the last Budget)
● another £20bn in tax avoidance
● and a further £80bn in tax evasion.

This is money taken from us all. And we can address this. Therefore I am announcing today that my fairer tax policies will include:

● The introduction of a proper anti-avoidance rule into UK tax law.
● The aim of country-by-country reporting for multinational corporations.
● Reform of small business taxation to discourage avoidance and tackle tax evasion.
● Enforce proper regulation of companies in the UK to ensure that they file their accounts and tax returns and pay the taxes that they owe.
● Lastly, and most importantly, a reversal of the cuts to staff in HMRC and at Companies House, taking on more staff at both, to ensure that HMRC can collect the taxes the country so badly needs.

George Osborne announced some modest extra funding for HMRC in his Budget, but this does not even reverse the cuts he made in the last Parliament. Tax justice is about creating a level playing field. Most of those reading this paper pay their taxes through PAYE - removed from their wages before they hit your bank account. You don't have fancy accountants routing your income through an offshore shell company; you cannot ask your boss to pay you in fine art or vintage wine to avoid your dues. You pay, so they should pay too.

My local coffee shop cannot pretend to buy its beans from a subsidiary to dishonestly shift its income to a low tax jurisdiction. When it makes money it pays its taxes fairly and on time. But how can it compete against a global multinational chain that engages in some of the most reprehensible practices?

Conclusion

We have a deeply unbalanced society, and a deeply unbalanced economy. We need a strategy for a more highly skilled, productive economy that works for the many not the few. The state has a vital strategic co-ordinating role to play in that. Without that role, we have the casino economy and the chaos of underinvestment, debt bubbles, and grotesque inequality between rich and poor, and a widening regional inequality.

Our vision is of an economy that works for all, provides opportunity for all, and invests in all – rich and poor, north, south, east and west. It means we judge our economy not by the presence of billionaires but by the absence of poverty; not only by whether GDP is rising, but by whether inequality is falling.

Labour must become the party of economic credibility AND economic justice

A more equal and more prosperous society that only a Labour government in 2020 can deliver.

II
Housing Policy
Tackling The Housing Crisis
August 2015

Introduction

A secure home is the foundation of a happy life and decent housing for all is the foundation of the good society. For too many people their housing is not a source of security, but a cause for anxiety.

The housing crisis cannot just be solved by building more homes, although this is a major issue that needs to be tackled. It is more complex than that: to tackle the housing crisis we also need to address problems of inequality, regional disparities of income and wealth, taxation policy, the labour market, our social security system and planning regulations.

There is a housing crisis in Britain – and this is a humanitarian crisis: homelessness, overcrowding, poor quality housing affecting people's health, young people not being able to afford to leave home and live independently. This crisis is getting worse:

● People are being priced out of home ownership: A first time buyer today requires ten times the deposit they did in the 1980s, according to the National Housing Federation.

● House building has dropped to record low levels: fewer than 150,000 homes were built in every year of the Coalition Government, compared with 190,000 homes a year under New Labour, which was itself a low for a post-war government.

● Rents are unaffordable: Britain has the highest proportion of households of OECD countries receiving cash allowances to support rent, and we now spend around £10 billion on housing benefit for in-work households; and the eviction of tenants is at a record high.

● Homelessness is rising: official figures show that sleeping rough in England is up 55% since 2010 (and up 78% in London); while families in temporary accommodation are increasing too. Labour will not win until the electorate are confident that we have the conviction and the policies to address the housing crisis.

This document assesses the main issues that need to be addressed in housing policy and attempts to set out the key policy measures required to deal with the housing crisis. Our aim must be to ensure that a secure home is a basic right – that is something that we as a society are capable of delivering for all.

Jeremy Corbyn MP

Councils and public investment to buil the homes we need

It is essential for councils to build if we're going to build the number of homes we need. We need to make sure we're building council homes and homes that first-time buyers can afford – not just high-value assets for global investors. A free-market free-for-all has simply failed to deliver this.

Evidence suggests that we need to be building at least 240,000 homes per year (the Coalition Government averaged 145,000). We should be meeting and building in excess of that target, with at least half comprising of council homes.

In London, where the housing crisis is most acute, we need to build at least 60,000 new homes a year. Under Boris Johnson and the Conservatives we are barely hitting half that number.

The most strongly supported measure to tackle London's housing crisis in a YouGov poll in April 2014 was to encourage London councils to build more social housing, with two-thirds of respondents being in support.

A National Investment Bank could support new build housing projects with low interest rates, both by councils and developers as long as tough new conditions were met on the proportion of genuinely affordable housing built. For every £1 spent on housing construction an extra £2.09 is generated in the economy.

Lifting the borrowing cap in the Housing Revenue Account would mean local authorities could borrow up to the prudential limits and thereby build more homes. Building the homes to meet the need would create thousands of skilled jobs across the country, and offer thousands of young people high quality apprenticeships.

We must also return to having regional home building targets to ensure homes are built in every area, so that rural areas benefit from building council homes as well as our urban centres.

A private rented sector that's fit for purpose

Alongside building the thousands of new homes we need, we also need to get rents down in the private rented sector and ensure secure tenures. We could have national minimum standards of longer tenancies and limits on rent rises – but in places where the housing crisis is at its most acute, we need to go further.

We need to bring rents down to make sure they take up a lower proportion of people's income, and given that many people are likely to rent for longer and longer, we need to make sure tenants have the right to a longer tenancy. A survey by Survation in January this year showed fewer than 10% of British people are against mandatory legal limits on housing rents.

Regulation of private rents should be linked to what determines whether something is affordable. We should consider average earnings and in particular their rate of increase, not the market rate for housing.

Berlin now has powers to limit how far landlords raise rents for all new contracts – and early evidence suggests this is already bringing rents down in the city. Private landlords should be nationally registered and locally licensed, including a 'fit and proper' persons test, making sure that tenants' rights are respected and ensuring that decent homes standards – such as minimum safety standards, and being damp and pest free – are adhered to in the private rental sector.

Licensing and registration should be administered and enforced by the relevant local authority. Some councils including London boroughs and Oxford City Council have already done some positive work in this area with the powers currently available to them, and it has been effective in moving against some of the worst offender landlords.

Home ownership

In the early 1990s, nearly two-thirds of Britons aged between 25 and 34 owned their own home; it is now down to less than 45%. Home ownership levels have been falling ever since Margaret

Thatcher left office as a whole generation has been priced out.

By a range of measures, including building more housing overall, restricting subsidies to buy-to-let landlords, and regulating rental value, we can bring down house prices and make home ownership an affordable option for more people.

In many cases, one of the biggest pressures first-time buyers face is to save a deposit, particularly in high-value areas where house prices are rising fast and people are trapped having to pay fast-rising rents. We could help people caught in this trap, with an approach that incorporates some of the principles applied in schemes like rent-to-own or shared equity, where the government helps with a deposit and in the latter case retains a share in the property.

Right-to-Buy

Right-to-Buy (RTB), introduced by the Conservatives in 1980, has already resulted in a massive depletion of the social housing stock – over 1.7 million homes were sold off by 1992. In London over a third of leaseholders owning properties bought under right to buy do not live in their properties but let them out for commercial rent – often subsidised by housing benefit.

Since 2012, 29,505 more council homes have been sold off, with only 3,422 replaced. Yet the current government proposes to extend right-to-buy discounts of £100,000 to tenants in housing association properties.

The National Housing Federation rightly states that housing association tenants are people already living in good secure homes on some of the country's cheapest rents … To use public assets to gift over £100,000 to someone already living in a good quality home is deeply unfair. Extending right to buy in this way was also found to be unpopular with a majority of respondents in a poll conducted in London earlier this year.

Instead of extending the right to buy we should be reducing the harm it causes to our affordable housing stock. Local authorities in areas of high housing stress should be given the power to suspend right to buy in order to protect depleting social housing assets. There are many other steps we could take as well. It is essential we make sure receipts from right-to-buy remain in a local area and that genuine replacements are built – an aim the government has sorely missed. We could also reduce the discount.

We should also look at how to help private renters, since they are often paying much higher rents with less security and a less responsive landlord than housing association tenants. We could re-direct some of the £14 billion of tax reliefs received by private landlords to help struggling private tenants; this would of course include building new council homes and helping private tenants to overcome the deposit problem. We could also investigate whether some of this money could be used to fund a form of right-to-buy shared equity scheme to private tenants in cases when they are renting from large-scale landlords.

Forced sale of council houses

Our housing crisis is set to get a lot worse as a result of the government's plans to force councils to sell 'high-value' council homes on the open market when they become vacant. They want to do this, in part, to pay off housing associations who will be forced to offer right-to-buy discounts to their tenants.

The damage of this policy is illustrated in London, where many inner London boroughs could lose a third or more of their council homes as a result of this policy, which we know are likely to go to investors and speculators. It will put yet more pressure on privately-rented homes, particularly in parts of outer London, as people on lower incomes desperately find somewhere even vaguely near family or work that they can afford.

There is widespread agreement of councils from different political parties across the capital that this will cause huge social upset – from Labour councillors in Islington to Conservative councillors in Kensington. Businesses too are saying that the lack of affordable housing threatens London's future economic success – four in five London employers say the lack of affordable housing is stalling economic growth in the capital. It is vital that communities and businesses in major cities like London oppose this damaging and reckless policy.

'Affordable' rents

We need to be clear what we mean by 'affordable' – no longer should 'affordable' mean near-market levels under the doublespeak the government has promoted.

Social rents in high-demand areas are typically a third to half the market rate, while so-called 'affordable' rents are up to 80% of private rents.

The government's new Pay to Stay policy, which from 2017 will force social tenant households earning over £30,000 (£40,000 in London) to pay market rents, will deter residents from seeking promotion at work, and encourage them to go for right-to-buy. The extra income from housing association tenants will be kept by the landlord, whilst the income from council tenants will go to the Treasury.

Pay to Stay will have a devastating impact on people, particularly in London and other inner city areas – forcing people from their homes just for earning over a certain amount, or possibly giving people a perverse incentive not to earn more if they have the option. It will undoubtedly come at the cost of building more homes for social rent in the current climate.

And there is a problem with housing associations. Initially set up to provide decent homes for people in need, many are developing into businesses that sell or rent at market levels. We need more democracy and accountability, and a return to their original purpose.

Instead of giving tenants in housing association property the right to buy, we should look at giving tenants greater power over the decisions their landlords take – including for instance through co-operative models of local management that can empower tenants.

Landbanking and speculative planning applications

Even in areas of acute housing shortage there is land that has planning permission but is not being developed. This is known as landbanking – a practice that Conservative London Mayor Boris Johnson has described as 'pernicious'.

We should consider introducing a Land Value Tax on

undeveloped land that has planning permission, and 'use it or lose it' measures on other brownfield sites, to act as a disincentive to landbanking and to raise public funds for house-building. Councils should also be allowed to compulsorily purchase (CPO) sites at a fair value if their owners are not developing them.

According to the Local Government Association, there are 709,426 empty properties in England. About one third of these, around 260,000, have been lying empty for six months or more. With home ownership becoming increasingly unattainable for so many, rents spiralling out of control and levels of homelessness rapidly increasing, working with local authorities, more should be done to bring existing housing stock back into use.

'Buy-to-leave'/off-plan sales

London is home to people from all around the world – its diversity and global attractiveness is one of its key strengths. This strength comes from people making it the place they live and work in.

Too many new homes that are built for sale end up as buy-to-let investments, or even worse as speculative assets that sit there empty for much of the year.

Many other cities around the world have taken steps to ensure homes go to people who live and work in the city rather than to people who see the homes as assets for financial peculation. Highly populated cities like Hong Kong and Singapore have taken steps to discourage overseas buyers.

Whilst ending this would by no means solve our housing crisis, it would play a part in a broader approach. Local authorities could be given the option of levying higher council tax rates or a new tax on properties left empty. Additionally we could look at banning the ownership of property by non-UK based entities or by companies and offshore trusts altogether.

Public land used for affordable homes

Boris Johnson and George Osborne have set out to produce a 'doomsday book' of public land in London that can be used for development, through a 'London Land Commission' being run by Savills estate agency. This does not include council-owned land but does include other public bodies e.g. the NHS.

There is a danger that the government see these land disposals simply as a way to raise as much money as possible, and with no provision for genuinely affordable housing. This public land should be developed in many cases, but should be transferred to councils to build council housing to meet local need.

Planning laws

Developers will nearly always argue for the release of green belt land because it is easier for them compared to developing brownfield sites. But we don't simply want our towns sprawling outwards with reliance on cars growing – and the green belt has prevented that to a certain extent. Any widespread relaxations would also risk inflating the land values of green belt sites, without careful planning requirements being set in place first.

The government's extended permitted development rights are also problematic and must be reversed. By not needing planning permission there cannot be an assessment and provision for the wider facilities and infrastructure that communities need. In residential conversions this of course includes affordable housing. It also includes transport, education, health facilities, leisure centres, green spaces, community centres, libraries and entertainment – all the things that bring people together in local areas to create sustainable communities.

Retrofitting and raising environmental standards

Britain needs more energy efficient housing – both in current housing stock and new build. It means ensuring all homes are properly insulated. The model for this should be the Warm Zones approach of Kirklees council (between 2007-2010) which installed loft and cavity wall insulation across the Borough, for free.

We also need new incentives – and obligations – to raise housing standards in the worst parts of the private rented sector.

Over 3.5 million people in Britain live in fuel poverty. Excess winter deaths are 23% higher than in Sweden, despite our milder winters. Retrofitting homes will reduce this toll of ill-health, unnecessary deaths and avoidable carbon emissions.

There is no excuse for Britain setting lower standards of new housing than elsewhere in Europe. Zero carbon homes should become the norm. France now requires even commercial buildings to have roofs covered in either plants or solar panels. Germany uses its equivalent of the Green Investment Bank to drive (and de-risk) high energy efficiency standards. Denmark will not accept planning applications for new buildings dependant on fossil fuels. The Netherlands requires buildings to be flood-resistant. Britain needs to future-proof its housing standards.

Local authorities must also be given greater freedoms to drive this change, underpinned by a shift in tax advantages/allowances in favour of energy efficient homes rather than subsidies to poor and unoccupied properties.

Social security

Reforms to welfare policy are increasingly leading to an exacerbated housing crisis, and causing the social cleansing of many cities.

The bedroom tax and the benefit cap should be scrapped. They penalise the tenant for the failure of government to build sufficient housing and to regulate rents.

This failing labour market is costing us all; the number of people in work claiming housing benefit to pay their rent has trebled since the crash despite George Osborne slashing entitlement to housing benefit, including through the bedroom tax and benefit cap. Spending on housing benefit has risen by 15% since 2010/11 to nearly £25 billion today, because wages are not enough to pay the rent.

It is clear the best way to bring down the benefits bill is through growth; we need more investment in the economy to provide the skilled jobs that can command better pay. There is a strong case for capping costs – but it is rents that should be capped. By capping rent levels, we will also save on housing benefit costs.

Our cities need to be affordable for all, with mixed communities, reflecting the fact every part of the country needs cleaners, bus drivers, teachers and nurses – pricing them out will only damage our society and our economy.

The UK economy has seen higher levels of net migration in

recent years (300,000 last year, up from 250,000 in 2010). Migrants have contributed immensely to our economy and society. Research from University College London shows that immigration has made a net contribution of around £25 billion to our economy.

It is the responsibility of Government to ensure that we are building sufficient housing to meet everyone's needs. This responsibility is not currently being met. Through their repeated failure to invest in housing the Conservatives and the previous Coalition Government have exacerbated the housing crisis.

We as a Labour Party must be bold in our vision to meaningfully address the housing crisis in Britain today.

Regional economic strategies

In many areas of the country, the housing crisis is much less acute and there are large numbers of vacant properties or swathes of residential land that has lain undeveloped for many years. The demand for housing is closely correlated with the supply of jobs, and a lack of investment in many parts of the country – and the absence of any regional economic strategy to develop high skilled work in those areas – means that there is acute overcrowding in some parts of the country, while there is massive underutilisation and 'brain drain' in others. By rebalancing our economy and investment throughout the UK we can ensure that all parts of the country provide decent work and that housing is utilised as efficiently as possible.

Conclusion

As with so many other policy areas, housing requires joined up policy between government departments, working with devolved government and local councils. The free market free-for-all in housing has failed. Only the government is able to play the strategic, co-ordinating role to tackle the housing crisis. This discussion document sets out some of the problems and attempts to outline some solutions. Your input would be welcome – in fact without it Labour will not get its housing policy right. As well as campaigning for a more rational housing policy, this campaign is about a more rational policy-making process.

III

Defence Diversification

August 2015

Introduction

I entered the Labour leadership contest as a candidate who is opposed to austerity, because it is possible to have investment to grow our economy and create decent jobs for all with a more equitable distribution of wealth. That is the central choice in the leadership election and the one facing Britain. Job security in high skill, high paid, productive work is not just good for those workers who have it, but good for our economy too.

I am committed to ensure that in transitioning away from nuclear weapons, we do so in a way that protects the jobs and skills of those who currently work on Trident, and in the defence sector more widely. This will help grow the British economy. The UK desperately needs to build its skills base and to invest in the industries that will take our country forward. That is why I have set out plans for both a National Education Service and for a National Investment Bank.

For all these reasons, I have set out a clear commitment to establishing a Defence Diversification Agency to focus on a ensuring a just transition for communities whose livelihoods are based in those sectors, so that engineering and scientific skills are not lost, but are transferred into more socially productive industries.

A huge investment in renewable energy networks, new and improved railway infrastructure, new housing, as well as upgrading our digital infrastructure are all necessary parts of that plan and will offer skilled job opportunities to those in the defence sector.

Additionally, the workforce in the defence industry will also have ideas about how the innovations you work on, and the skills you have, can be adapted to other social uses.

So a Defence Diversification Agency should not be some arcane Whitehall bureaucracy, but will be driven by the workforce and communities in partnership with government. We need a strategy to redeploy those skills to tasks that will build a stronger country for all and these are the issues that a DDA would be tasked with taking forward in practical terms.

From energy to the railways, from housing to digital infrastructure, the UK lags behind the rest of the world in our infrastructure. In Britain we do not lack the innovators or inventors, but we do lack the strategic government and public investment to support them, and to harness their skills and insights. Money saved by not replacing our nuclear weapons system could be used to sustain the process of defence diversification, vital to our manufacturing future, as well as freeing resources for investment in other socially-useful forms of public spending to build a sustainable future that benefits us all. I am confident that we can make a just transition to a nuclear-weapons free Britain, and diversify more of the skills in the defence sector into more peaceful industries.

Timelines

In 2016, Parliament is expected to vote on Trident renewal. With a Conservative majority government it is unfortunately possible that such a vote will pass.

The next general election will take place in 2020. If a Labour government is elected committed to ending Trident renewal then we will enter government with a plan – discussed and agreed with communities, workforce, trade unions and industries affected over the next five years – for protecting skills and diversifying work so that no jobs or skills are lost.

Within the wider context of a new industrial policy, there will be investment to create more skilled science, engineering and technology roles.

Jobs and communities

Currently, across the country there are many thousands of workers who rely on the civil and naval nuclear programmes for their jobs and for retention and development of skill across many sectors. These include shipbuilding, aerospace, transport, mechanical and electrical design, project management and IT, as well as many more in the supporting supply chains.

If we look at the figures, Trident is estimated by the BASIC

Trident Commission to cost £83.7 billion between 2016 to 2062, equivalent to £1.86 billion a year. At a total employment cost of £60,000 a year that annual expenditure would sustain 31,000 jobs. By contrast it is estimated that Trident currently sustains 11,000 jobs. For this level of investment, we should be creating far more jobs.

However, in some areas of the country Trident (and the wider defence sector) can be major employers – for example Barrow-in-Furness, Devonport and Rosyth. Commitments need to be made to not just maintain, but to increase skilled jobs in those areas, many of which currently suffer from higher than average unemployment.

It is projected that decommissioning the existing Trident system under the 'Submarine Dismantling Project' will take 60 years – and so some jobs will remain in the industry for decades to come. We can also maintain jobs in the wider defence sector by ensuring Britain's legitimate defence equipment needs are met from domestic producers, through better procurement policies.

The National Investment Bank, working with government departments, should have the mandate to invest to ensure that skilled manufacturing and construction jobs in areas like renewable energy and housing outnumber those lost in the defence sector, and are located in areas with a high density of existing defence work.

When the Tory government of the 1980s de-industrialised the North, and indeed many other parts of the country too, they allowed unemployment to increase sharply to very high levels, which became entrenched. Now the Conservative government's austerity programme has squeezed defence budgets and cut spending on conventional defence and conventional defence manufacturing jobs, while maintaining its commitment to Trident replacement.

We are proposing a careful strategy – backed by investment – to ensure a just transition, as part of an industrial policy committed to more high skill manufacturing jobs.

Defence diversification

Defence diversification is about working with workers in the defence industry to identify how the skills they have and technology they work on can be put to more socially productive use.

I have proposed that a Defence Diversification Agency (DDA) is established – jointly between workers, industry and government to ensure that jobs and skills are not just maintained, but also expanded.

Defence sector research and innovation has led to many advances we all take for granted today. As Professor Mariana Mazzucato has pointed out, if you take your smartphone, the touch-screen technology, GPS, the internet and voice activation – the things that make a smartphone smart – were all publicly funded, mostly for the military.

Working in partnership between the industry, the workforce, the national investment bank and expertise from our universities, we can ensure that innovations can be explored and developed to maintain high skilled jobs. Many facilities in the US have successfully made the transition to a post-nuclear age, following the end of the Cold War, when funding was cut back. The UK government would need to learn best practice from these and other experiences worldwide.

Additionally, working alongside the National Investment Bank, the DDA can help those with transferable skills move into other high skill roles in the growing energy, housebuilding, and digital industries. It is only a progressive government with an industrial investment strategy that can manage this transition while not only protecting jobs and communities, but also improving skills and job prospects.

The case against nuclear weapons

We are making the case for a Defence Diversification Agency because we have a moral duty, and strategic defence and international commitments, to make Britain and the world a safer place. As a signatory to the Nuclear Non-Proliferation Treaty, Britain should therefore give a lead in discharging its obligations by not seeking a replacement for Trident, as we are committed to 'accelerate concrete progress' towards nuclear disarmament .

Senior military figures have described our existing nuclear weapons as 'militarily useless'; and our possession of them encourages other countries to seek a similar arsenal while undermining the efforts being made to advance the cause of international nuclear disarmament.

Many trade unions with members working in the defence sector oppose Trident renewal – including Unite, PCS and FDA. In 2013 the TUC Congress confirmed its opposition too.

Conclusion and further reading

In opposition, Labour should be working with communities, employees, their unions, industry and academic expertise to prepare a programme ready for implementation from May 2020 that protects skills and jobs in the defence sector, while ensuring a just transition to a post-nuclear weapons age.

Considerable research has already been undertaken in the field of defence diversification and looking at the possible approaches, and the impact and options of not renewing Trident. Some particularly useful studies are listed below:

- Trident & Jobs - the case for Scottish Defence Diversification Agency STUC, 2014
- 'Trident Alternatives Review and the future of Barrow' Nuclear Education Trust, December 2012
- 'Defence-Industrial Issues: Employment, Skills, Technology and Regional Impacts' BASIC Trident Commission, March 2012
- 'Trident, Jobs and the UK economy - a briefing by the Campaign for Nuclear Disarmament' CND, September 2010
- 'Cancelling Trident: The economic and employment consequences for Scotland' SCND/STUC, 2007

IV

Protecting our Planet

August 2015

Introduction

The Labour movement and environmental movement are natural allies. We are fighting for the same thing: for society to be run in our collective interests and in the interests of protecting our planet. Promoting the well being of our planet, its people and ecosystems must be at the heart of the Labour Party's vision of a fairer, more prosperous future.

There is an electoral dimension. To win, we must show we have a modern vision of an innovative country that has a new idea of prosperity and success. Our collective aspirations must lie with a greener vision of Britain. And we must reach out to those voters who care deeply about the environment if we are to build the electoral alliance we need.

Climate change is a threat to our very existence. Tackling climate change will only be effective if social justice is at the heart of the solutions we propose. Pope Francis recently said:

> *We are faced not with two separate crises, one environmental and the other social, but rather with one complex crisis which is both social and environmental. Strategies for a solution demand an integrated approach to combating poverty, restoring dignity to the excluded, and at the same time protecting nature.*

Despite claiming to lead the 'greenest government ever', David Cameron's Conservatives have reverted to protecting the entrenched short-term interests of the minority who have benefited through the unsustainable exploitation of the Earth's resources and people.

It is a scandal that six million households are seriously struggling to pay their energy bills. 29,000 people die early every year because of polluted air. Already 5 million people are at risk of their homes being flooded. Children are growing up without contact with nature or access to green spaces that are so important for development.

The things we need to do to protect the environment also protect people and enhance our lives. As Labour leader I would bring together a coalition of the majority, to move on from a wasteful, polluting and unequal economic approach to our environment and instead democratise our economy to reduce inequality and promote sustainable development within the Earth's resource limits.

Our campaign will prioritise our planet and stand for:

- Britain providing international leadership on climate change and the socialisation of our energy supply leading to an end to the era of fossil fuels.
- A modern, green, resource-efficient economy – creating one million new climate jobs.
- Ensuring everyone has access to a decent home that is low-carbon and affordable to keep warm.
- Putting people and planet first – tackling the cost of living and climate crisis together.
- Cleaner air – tackling the air pollution crisis in our big cities and committing to full independent public inquiry into levels of air pollution.
- Protecting our ecosystems, wildlife habitats and a compassionate approach to animal welfare.
- An international approach – support internationally agreed, universal standards of regulation of emissions and pollution.
- A healthy, safe environment, where people and nature thrive together.

Climate change

For four decades scientists have known that emissions from fossil fuels are causing the climate to change in a dangerous way. The world has already warmed 0.8 degrees causing hundreds of thousands of people to suffer food shortages and extreme weather, from increased droughts in the Sahara, to typhoons in the Philippines and floods in Britain.

Without urgent action to get off fossil fuels, the world is on track for at least 4 degrees of warming by the end of the century, which would see millions of climate refugees as large parts of the world become uninhabitable, with increased conflict not just for oil, but for food and fresh water.

The science is clear. To have a chance of remaining under the 2 degree 'tipping point', 80% of the world's known fossil fuel reserves must stay in the ground. Global emissions must start to decline within the next 5 years – by 2020. Institutions from the Rockefeller Foundation to the Norwegian Sovereign Wealth Fund have started divesting.

Instead of shifting Britain's energy supply from the fuels that are driving climate change, the Tory Government has committed the UK in law to 'maximise the economic exploitation of fossil fuels' – a position previously backed by Labour. In the last Parliament, the Tories spent £3 billion on fossil fuel subsidies and blocked renewable energy targets for Europe. George Osborne said the Government is going 'all out for fracking' and has recently introduced regulation that would allow fracking in national parks and through aquifers, risking contaminating the water we drink.

We in the Labour Party must stand for a different Britain that would play a leading role internationally – committed to cutting our fair share of carbon emissions and driving international support for a fossil-fuel-free future. We must fundamentally challenge a Conservative government that is already racing in pursuit of an environmentally devastating agenda. As the Paris Summit approaches, this Conservative government's approach must be challenged.

With London's air quality already at damaging levels, regularly exceeding EU legal limits, the government has made it £1,000 more expensive to buy a low-carbon car than a more polluting one. Despite the UK having the highest levels of fuel poverty in Europe, the government has proceeded with dumping the Green Deal, in favour of no deal at all. With the world demanding we find ways of 'leaving carbon in the ground', this Government has cut renewables investment while supporting fracking and offering new incentives to offshore oil.

While continuing to fund tax allowances for energy companies, the government has levied a carbon tax on the only sources of energy not emitting carbon. The IMF has reported that Britain throws seven times more subsidies at the fossil fuel industry than it puts into renewable energy (£26 billion last year, as against £3.5 billion going to renewables).

Urgent, meaningful action to address climate change is long overdue. Labour must put policies for sustainability at the heart of everything we do. We must put forward a Labour vision of a more prosperous, fairer and greener future.

Our vision

Leading the energy revolution

At the core of our environmental pledge is a radical restructuring of Britain's dated, inefficient and polluting energy market. My overarching commitment will be for Britain to take the lead in developing the clean energy economy of the future. Over the next few decades 8 countries, 55 cities and 60 regions are aiming to have 100% renewable electricity, heating/cooling and/or transport systems. This is what a sustainable future will look like. Britain must be a part of it.

Socialising our energy supply

A typical household in Germany can choose to buy its energy from over 70 different suppliers (out of a national total of over 1,100).

Half of German energy suppliers are owned by local authorities, communities and small businesses. There are now over 180 German towns and cities taking over their local electricity grids, selling themselves cleaner (and cheaper) electricity they increasingly produce for themselves. It would (currently) be illegal to do so in the UK. While Britain has over 95% of our electricity market controlled by the Big 6, Germany has almost 2 million electricity generators. Germany's Big 4 control just 5% of their clean energy market. The majority is owned by households, farmers, communities and localities. In the three decades since privatisation in the UK, the big energy companies have failed to invest in the energy infrastructure we need, and have instead sweated the public assets they were handed. They have made record profits while energy bills have been driven sky high. Britain needs an energy policy for the Big 60 million not the Big 6.

I pledge, if elected Leader of the Labour Party, to meet the challenge of climate change with ten energy pledges to reform our broken, dated and polluting energy market.

Energy Pledges

1) My over-arching commitment will be for Britain to take the lead in developing the clean Energy Economy of the future.

2) As leader I would establish an Energy Commission to draft a fundamental shift in UK energy thinking.

3) The Commission will be tasked to produce a route-map into tomorrow's 'smart energy' systems that will:

● Deliver more, but consume less;
● Use clean energy before dirty;
● Put energy saving before more consumption;
● Use smart technologies to run localised storage, balancing and distribution mechanisms;
● Shift the costs of grid access and grid balancing from clean energy across to dirty;
● Be open, democratic, sustainable and accountable (in ways that today's market is not).

4) The Commission will be charged with bringing new partners into energy policy making. These will include local authorities, communities, energy co-operatives, and 'smart' technology companies that are already working on tomorrow's 'virtual' power systems and new energy thinking.

5) As leader I will conduct a root and branch review of energy market subsidies; moving away from the notion of everlasting hand-outs; instead, using public support as 'transition funding' that transforms Britain's energy infrastructure.

6) I will expect the energy industry, not the public, to meet the costs of their own clean-up.

7) I will look to re-define the roles of Ofgem, National Grid and the Competition and Markets Authority, to promote a more genuinely open, competitive and sustainable energy market; one in which there are more players and more clean energy choices than we have today.

8) I will examine ways to allow communities to be owners of local energy systems, with the right (as in other parts of Europe) to have first use of the energy they generate themselves.

9) We must socialise our energy supply and move toward breaking up the failing energy cartel. Instead, I want to look at the role of the

state as guarantor of last resort; with more direct responsibility for the nation's back-up generation, high voltage grid and interconnectors; directly ensuring that Britain's 'lights never go out'.

10) I would commit Britain to binding international climate change commitments; making national targets, local ones too, and devolving both the necessary powers and duties to meet these obligations.

This is now a necessity, not a utopian dream. Britain must lead the way in developing the energy systems of the future.

Tackling climate change

If we are going to make meaningful progress in tackling climate change, we must make meaningful, bold commitments to doing so.

Britain should commit to playing a leading role in getting the world on track to climate safety – with the UK cutting our fair share of carbon at home.

We must take action now to keep fossil fuels in the ground – end dirty energy handouts, ban fracking and set a target date to end new fossil fuel extraction, and begin to phase out high polluting coal power stations with support for workers to re-train. Britain should scrap the 'capacity market' which subsidises coal, gas and nuclear power at greater expense.

Investing in our future: A green investment bank

Germany's equivalent Development Bank loans money (at 1% interest) to support their Transformation programme – including energy efficient homes. They also simplify and de-risk the shift into clean energy living. If Germany can do this, so can Britain. We need a National Investment Bank, with the power to borrow to boost our green economy, supporting the green jobs, homes and infrastructure of the future. Britain has the largest renewable energy potential in Europe. Using just one-third of our offshore wind, wave and tidal energy potential would make Britain a net exporter of electricity.

275,000 people already work in renewable energy in Britain, and renewables already generate nearly a fifth of our electricity. Under Tory cuts to solar, wind and home insulation programmes, green projects are being scrapped along with their potential for jobs.

Investment in a green future could establish a manufacturing base of the future, rebalance our economy and create a million high-skilled jobs. Renewable energy supports more jobs than fossil fuels. With the right support, we could develop the new high-tech manufacturing hubs of the future across Britain that build on the expertise of our universities.

We should boost support for renewable energy – setting out a road map to a million climate jobs and new green high-tech manufacturing hubs in all parts of Britain.

By setting a bold target of carbon-free electricity by 2030, reversing the Tories' ideological restrictions on renewable energy projects (onshore wind and large solar), investing in low-emission transport and establishing a National Investment Bank, we can deliver the changes needed to secure the future prosperity of our people and planet.

A cleaner more efficent model:
Tackling the cost of living and the climate crisis together

Too many people are struggling to pay their energy bills and have no choice but to spend too much of their income on travelling. It is a national scandal that each year people are suffering and dying from cold-related illnesses due to living in a cold home they could not afford to heat. 29,000 people died prematurely because of air pollution primarily caused by transport fumes. This is not acceptable and we must therefore pledge to both reduce carbon emissions and bring down the cost of living. The cost of solar has fallen 70% since 2009, and onshore wind is even cheaper. It is estimated carbon-free power would cost bill payers £23 billion less than relying on gas.

Zero carbon homes must become the norm, not the exception. To achieve this requires both higher energy efficiency standards on all new builds, while maintaining planning regulations protecting our greenbelt, as well as a national home insulation programme that would save the average household £250 on their energy bill, and cut carbon emissions.

Half a million households now benefit from free energy provided by solar panels, thanks to the last Labour Government's scheme to support household and community solar. This should be extended. A radical commitment to energy efficiency policies would both create jobs and save lives. It can be driven, in part, by regulation and taxation, but also by energy market reform; allowing localities to 'sell' energy saving in preference to more consumption.

Investment in public transport will both reduce fares and reduce car use, as well as halting the rise of asthma and other preventable air pollution diseases, potentially saving the NHS £18 billion in treated illness caused by air pollution.

Protecting our ecosystems

A healthy and safe environment where people and nature thrive

Nature is in trouble. The Earth has lost half its wildlife in the last 40 years. Species across land, rivers and seas are being decimated by pollution, habitat loss, the impacts of climate change, and being killed in unsustainable numbers for food.

The British bee population is in crisis, and England has the greatest decline of anywhere in Europe. Banning neonicotinoid pesticides that are harmful to bees and pollinators must be a priority as part of a multi-faceted approach to protecting our bee population and ecosystems more broadly.

Equally we must protect our oceans, tackling water pollution and revisiting legal limits of fish extraction and fishing protections.

People must also be protected from the climate change we cannot avoid. The winter floods of 2013/14 took place in the wettest winter since records began 250 years ago – with devastating flooding affecting huge swathes of the country. Without action, research shows that the impact of climate change and population growth would mean a million more people in the UK could be at significant risk of flooding by the 2020s. Flood defences should not be cut, flood plains should be protected, and the non-permeable paving of permeable spaces must be looked into it.

I am opposed to fracking and to new nuclear on the basis of the dangers posed to our ecosystems.

Fracking will accelerate climate change, carries significant pollution risks and deepen our dependency on polluting fossil fuels, as well as preventing investment in the clean energy sources we need.

New nuclear power will mean the continued production of dangerous nuclear waste and an increased risk from radioactive accident and nuclear proliferation. In May, Sellafield nuclear waste site in Cumbria was granted permission to exceed legal limits for the amount of hot radioactive waste it can keep in tanks, following an accident that has led to a backlog of waste. The government plans to subsidise new nuclear power plants to the tune of £77 billion, despite the cost of cleaning up the existing nuclear waste reaching £100 billion.

Instead we should be looking at more sustainable solutions to the ways in which we deliver answers to the transport, heating, cooling and power needs in a society that must live more lightly on the planet. It is the only one we've got. We must clean up our act, clean up our air and clean up our mess all at the same time.

Internationally, differing standards of emissions and pollution regulations have led to the effective out-sourcing of pollution and emissions to countries with more lax environmental enforcement. We as an international community must bring an end to this practice and work towards universal standards of pollution and emissions regulations in order to protect our planet. This also means rejecting the Transatlantic Trade and Investment Partnership (TTIP) agreement.

Conclusion

A sustainable and compassionate approach to protecting our environment must be at the heart of everything we as a Labour Party propose to the British electorate. Some 200 years ago Britain led the world into the last energy revolution. Our first 'public' energy company was formed in Manchester back in 1817. Having led the way into the last energy revolution we are now lagging behind in the current one. Technologies that have revolutionised the telecommunications sector are about to do the same to energy; making energy systems more open and competitive, and more sustainable and democratic. It isn't too late for Britain to catch up, and even lead, this energy revolution.

Until 1947, most of Britain's energy companies were municipal ones; with utility services providing local councils with 50% of their total income. Tomorrow's smart towns, cities and regions are already looking at using today's technologies (of energy generation storage, sharing and saving) to do the same. This is the Britain I want to build: a future that is innovative, inclusive and sustainable.

Contributors

Jeremy Corbyn is the Leader of the Labour Party.

Umaar Kazmi is a Labour Party activist, studying Law and Spanish at the University of Nottingham.

Abi Rhodes works for the Bertrand Russell Peace Foundation and studies politics and critical theory at the University of Nottingham.

Ben Sellers is a member of Red Labour's organising group and runs The People's Bookshop in Durham.

Christine Shawcroft is a long-serving member of the Labour Party's National Executive Committee, and contributes to *Labour Briefing.*

Tony Simpson edits *The Spokesman,* journal of the Bertrand Russell Peace Foundation, and is a member of UNITE.

Tom Unterrainer teaches mathematics and is compiling a political bibliography of Ken Coates, who helped establish the Institute for Workers' Control.

Nadia Whittome is Youth Officer of Rushcliffe CLP and an active young member of GMB, Unite Community and Nottingham People's Assembly

Adele Williams is Secretary of Sherwood Branch Labour Party in Nottingham East CLP and a trade union administrator.

Chris Williamson, former Labour MP for Derby North, lost his seat by 41 votes at the 2015 General Election. Chris is a regular contributor to *Tribune* and spoke on behalf of Jeremy Corbyn's campaign at meetings across the country.